CALIFORNIA HEARTLAND

Above: A.H. Hewitt and daughter, Inez, circa 1890. Inez Hewitt is the mother of a local journalist, Jane Ellis. Courtesy Special Collection, Meriam Library, California State University, Chico (SC 9837).

CALIFORNIA HEARTLAND

A PICTORIAL HISTORY AND TOUR GUIDE
OF EIGHT NORTHERN CALIFORNIA COUNTIES
Yuba, Sutter, Colusa, Glenn, Butte, Nevada, Sierra, Plumas

BY SANDRA BRUBAKER SHEPHERD

SCOTTWALL ASSOCIATES, PUBLISHERS
SAN FRANCISCO
1993

Book design: James Heig and Suzie Kirrane
Cover design: James Heig

First Edition: 5 4 3 2 1
Copyright ©1993 Sandra Brubaker Shepherd

Published November 1993
Scottwall Associates, Publishers
95 Scott Street
San Francisco, CA 94117
Telephone (415)861-1956

Printed in the U.S.A.

ISBN 0-942087-07-0

To the memory
of my beloved father, George William Brubaker
and brother, Thomas George Brubaker,
I dedicate this book

Acknowledgments

To all the organizations, Chambers of Commerce, libraries and their staffs, museum curators and staffs, I thank each of you for your valuable contributions.
Beale Air Force Base, Public Affairs Office
Butte County Historical Society
California State University, Chico, Meriam Library, Special Collections
California State Library, California Section
Community Memorial Museum, Yuba City
Lost Sierras Association
Marysville and Oroville Post Offices
Mary Aaron Museum, Marysville
Nevada County Historical Society
Plumas County Museum, Quincy
Sacramento Valley Museum, Williams
Searls Historical Library and Museum
Sutter County Library, Yuba City
Willows Museum
Yuba County Library, Marysville
Yuba Feather Historical Association

I also want to thank the following people, who helped me obtain photographs or information, or who gave their moral support:
Otto Becker, Sutter
Jo Brubaker Cason, Live Oak
Jerry Cooper, Loma Rica
Charles Gentles, Oroville
Jim Johnson, Heritage Graphics, Grass Valley
Jon Kitchen
Jim Lague, Oroville
Marion McElroy, Live Oak
Mike Miller, Alleghany
Jim Morgan, Forbestown
Bob Nation, Maxwell
Evelyn Nesmith, Los Angeles
John Nopel, Chico
Marc Ockerman, Yuba City
Dorothy Page, Yuba City
William Peardon, Smartville
Harold Peterson, Arbuckle
Phil Shepherd, Sutter
Gloria Walchesky, Sutter
Fred Ziegenmeyer, Sutter
Postal employees: Eileen Haney, Lynn Longway, Clint Powell, Betty Taylor, and Frank Yamamoto
To my publisher and editor, James Heig, go my very special gratitude and applause.

INTRODUCTION

CALIFORNIA, THE GOLDEN LAND, has always attracted the pioneer, adventurer, home-steader, traveler, and creative dreamer. The rich soil, green meadows, rugged mountains, sun-bleached deserts, raging sea coasts, serene rivers and warm climate have drawn settlers to raise livestock, grow enormous varieties of crops, and exploit a wealth of natural resources: gold, copper, lead, gas, oil, and timber.

The discovery of gold in Coloma, California, in 1848 was the historical turning point which led to the settling of towns and farmland in the Northern Sacramento Valley and the surrounding foothills. The native Americans and the long-time Mexican residents soon were overwhelmed by the flood of outsiders who grasped for their chance at a piece of this golden valley. As more and more people arrived, mule trains and ox-carts gave way to steamboats pushing their way up the rivers to deliver goods and mail to ports that led to the mining trails. The river town of Marysville developed as the hub or gateway to the mining camps. Boom towns sprouted and went bust as the land was raped of its treasure. Permanent settlements grew more slowly as the railroads steamed across the fruitful land.

Agriculture produced a new kind of gold: peaches, apricots, citrus, almonds, walnuts, wheat. On these and other riches from the land the counties of the Northern Sacramento Valley—Yuba, Sutter, Colusa, Glenn, Butte, Nevada, Sierra and Plumas—built their fortunes, their histories and their futures.

California soon became an interwoven network of cultures, reminiscent of Grandmother's treasured "crazy quilt." Instant millionaires, worn-out miners, paupers, Christians, Buddhists, thieves, ministers, gamblers, doctors, land barons, businessmen, mule skinners, farmhands, and immigrants from the world over, all came to the northern valley, looking for their land of golden opportunity. This astonishing mixture of people became the citizens who pioneered the unique and quaint townships of the Northern Sacramento Valley and the foothills above it. Men and women worked hand in hand to build strong and thriving towns and villages—people like John and Annie Bidwell, the Kelsey brothers, Mike Nye, Captain C.M. Weber, Joseph Chiles, Josiah Belden. Some were members of the first emigrant party to come to California over the Sierras. Others sailed around the Horn, or crossed the Isthmus of Panama. They built with pride and ingenuity, if not always with foresight. They left their legacy on the land: place names, houses, hotels, schools, churches, commercial buildings, ranches.

My paternal grandfather, W.R. Brubaker, came to Live Oak in the early 1900s and left his mark on the little town. By the time I entered the world, my parents had put down deep roots there. My father's Sunday drives after church, without my realizing it at the time, lit a spark in my spirit, a yearning to travel, to explore new places, to relish the beauty of the countryside. Growing up in a small town, I learned to value civic pride, family closeness, and individualism. I was insatiably curious about the neighboring towns and their histories. Why had one community remained a rural hamlet, uncluttered and simple, while another town close by grew into a metropolis with overpopulation and traffic jams?

A career in the postal service gave me a chance to travel to the counties included in this pictorial guide. The more I traveled, the more my appetite was whetted for the stories of the towns and villages. I began collecting old photographs, having copies made of pictures from private collections, and eventually visiting the California State Library in Sacramento, the Meriam Library at Chico State University, and the California Room of the Yuba County Library in Marysville, all storehouses of superb vintage photographs. Finding those treasures led me to the small-town museums, where local history is often more alive, more immediate, because they contain the very stuff of the past: the everyday objects—clothing, tools, dishes, kitchen utensils, bits of finery, mementos—that earlier generations touched and used and wore out. I urge readers to visit these museums. Nothing gives a more vivid understanding of the quality of life in days gone by than inspecting a primitive washing machine, hefting an old flatiron, or holding a scythe whose handles are worn to fit the hand. Pictures and information from these museums were, of course, invaluable to me in preparing this book.

These photographs yield insight into the lives of our forefathers, telling us of their taste in clothing and architecture, their methods of travel, how they earned their living, what they were proud of, what moments in their lives they wanted to preserve in the days when having a picture made was no everyday occurrence. Stumbling onto surprising past events, fascinating folklore, and funny bits of information in conjunction with the wonderful old pictures, I came to feel my collection was far too precious to keep tucked away only for my own pleasure. At last I began assembling the pictures into a book in order to make them accessible to those who are unable to rummage through libraries, museums, and people's attics.

While the pictures help us to relive the exciting past of these towns, there is even more excitement in seeing for oneself the historic places and the great scenic beauty of the eight counties included in this book. My hope is that readers will use the book as a guide for travel, sightseeing and exploring. For this reason I have included maps as well as lists of events, points of interest, accommodations, and special attractions, grouped together under the heading "Resources," for each place. Residents of the eight counties can use this book to get to know their neighbors better. Visitors from further afield may follow their interest in history and adventure to discover an ideal vacation spot, or even a place to settle down.

Sandy Shepherd
Sutter, California, 1993

TABLE OF CONTENTS

Dunning Bros. Co. of Marysville, circa 1911. A food and mail delivery company. A note on the picture suggests that the station wagon was a Reo, built by R.E. Olds, who later made the Oldsmobile. The Dunning Brothers owned various businesses in Marysville in the early 1900s. Courtesy California Room, Yuba County Library, Marysville.

HALL & CRANDALL'S
LINE OF STAGES.

CARRYING THE U. S. MAIL,

LEAVES SACRAMENTO DAILY FOR

MARYSVILLE, TEHAMA,

RED BLUFFS, CAVERTSBURG,

ONE HORSE TOWN, MIDDLETOWN,

AND SHASTA.

FRENCH GULCH, TRINITY RIVER, WHISKY CREEK,

WEAVERVILLE, YREKA AND THE PITT RIVER DIGGINGS,

Landing passengers at all intermediate points.

FOR MARYSVILLE,

Three six-horse Stages leave and return daily. The public may rest assured that the arrangements of this line, for speed and comfort are unsurpassed in the world. Neither pains nor expense having been spared in procuring the BEST HORSES, finest CONCORD COACHES, and the most competent and CAREFUL DRIVERS.

For particulars of the times of departure, arrival, price of passage, &c., inquire of JOHN SADLEIR GRAHAM, Agent, office Crescent City Hotel, Sacramento, and at the respective offices along the line.

Advertisement for the stage lines serving Northern California in the 1850s.
Courtesy California Room, Yuba County Library, Marysville.

"THE HUB" AND ITS SURROUNDINGS

Above: Dredging crew sitting on a gear of a dredger in Hammonton. Courtesy California Room, Yuba County Library, Marysville.

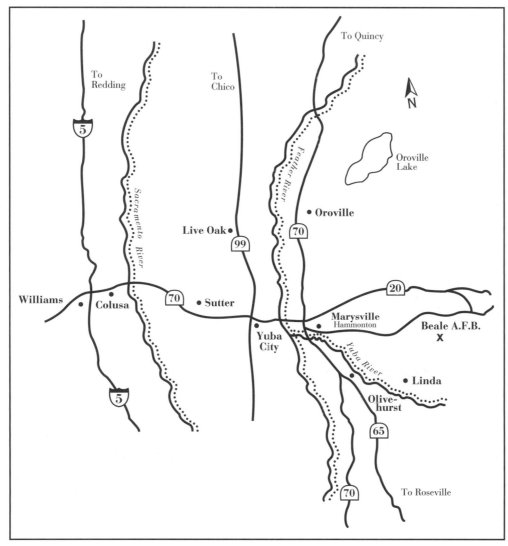

MARYSVILLE

For almost a century and a half, Marysville has been known as "The Hub" of the Sacramento Valley. It lies at the junction of the Yuba and Feather Rivers, approximately 50 miles north of Sacramento. The first buildings in town were of canvas stretched over wooden boards. After several fires swept through the tent town, buildings began being constructed of locally kilned bricks. The town's founder was Charles Covillaud, a former employee of Theodore Cordua, who bought half of Cordua's ranch. A year later, in 1849, he purchased the remaining parcel, known as "Nye's Ranch," from Michael C. Nye and William Foster. Charles Covillaud sold all but a fourth of the original Mexican land grant to Jose Ramirez, John Sampson and Theodore Sicard, but kept the prime land situated along the Feather River. He married Nye's sister-in-law, Mary Murphy, who had been a survivor of the fated Donner Party and for whom Marysville is named. By 1850 permanent residents numbered 500, while the floating population was about 1,000.

Steamers from Sacramento took almost seven hours for their bi-weekly trips to Marysville in the 1850s, but they made Marysville an important business center. Some $10 million in gold was shipped from the town's banks in 1857 alone. Steamers continued to navigate the river for three decades until debris from hydraulic mining made the river impassable in dry seasons. The queen city served as the head-out point to the gold diggings and surrounding farmlands. The roads leading to the northern mines were only trails worn by pack trains. At the height of the transport business, 50 pack trains with 4,000 horses and mules were boarded in Marysville.

Today with a population of 12,300, the town boasts many historic sites and landmarks, dated buildings and Victorian houses. A once bustling town with its mixture of immigrants, miners, gamblers, merchants, travelers and local town folk, Marysville now quietly awaits its revival as an important historic district.

A lithograph, circa 1850, depicts Marysville's River Dock, with boats bringing passengers and supplies from Sacramento. Courtesy California Room, Yuba County Library, Marysville.

Above: Downtown Marysville, looking north down D Street from 2nd Street, circa 1920. On the left corner of 2nd and D Streets is the Western Hotel. Schneider's Clothing Store, on the right side at 229 D Street, remained open for business until the 1980s. The Northern Electric train, serving Sacramento, Marysville and Colusa, runs down the middle of the street. Courtesy California Room, Yuba County Library, Marysville.

Left: A photograph from Griffith's "Elite Gallery" in Marysville depicts a couple of the 1880s. Author's Collection.

WHEN CALIFORNIA became a state in 1850, Marysville became the county seat of Yuba County, at that time encompassing today's Yuba, Nevada and Sierra Counties. Yuba County took its name from either the wild grapes growing along the river, which were called "uba" in Spanish, or the Yuba tribe of Maidu Indians living along the banks of the Feather River. Recorded history has not determined which derivation is correct.

WHEN THE DIGGINGS gave out, mining companies were formed to blast away whole mountainsides with water forced through high-pressure nozzles or "cannons". It is estimated that this hydraulic mining washed away six times as much earth as was moved to build the Panama Canal. Debris from hydraulic mining began to bury camps along the Yuba River with up to 200 feet of silt. There was so much sediment that the Yuba River bed rose above the level of the town of Marysville, resulting in many floods. Eventually the raised river beds prevented the steamers from making their way up the river from Sacramento. Agricultural lands along the Yuba and Bear Rivers were destroyed. Conflicts began to break out between the "flatlanders" and the mountain miners. Resulting law suits led to the famous Sawyer Decision of 1884, making the dumping of debris into rivers illegal.

Marysville, after its colorful beginnings, was destined to become a thriving and important community in the Sacramento Valley. Law and justice were desperately needed in the Northern country. In the earlier days people pretty much took justice in their own hands, and settled disputes with fists or pistols. Yuba County's Hank McCoy had a reputation for being one the greatest sheriffs in Northern California. This clever, calm and intelligent man, who stood 6'2", was known for "bringing back his man."

Marysville at one time ranked as the second largest city in California, second only to San Francisco. By 1853, the town fathers were meeting to nominate Marysville for the site of the State Capitol. When the site for the Capitol was awarded to Sacramento, Marysville soon fell to third position. Although this plan failed, the town can take pride in other accomplishments: The old Packard Library, across the street from the

Post Office, was the first free public library west of the Mississippi. The first "chain" banking system in California, the Rideout Banks, was founded by Marysville's Norman D. Rideout. Frederick Low of Marysville (1863) was the first governor of California to serve a four-year term.

Roland H. Macy, founder of New York's renowned department store, opened the very first Macy & Co. in Marysville in August of 1850, on the corner of 2nd Street and Maiden Lane (now Oak Street). Along with his brother Charles and two other partners, they accommodated the travelers. miners, and businessmen with clothes, supplies, etc. After only a couple of months in business, the partnership was dissolved and Roland returned to Massachusetts and later New York to reopen his mercantile business. Edward W. Tracy bought the business while Charles Macy remained in Marysville, where he died in 1856 and was laid to rest in the town's cemetery.

The hanging of Ah Ben, a Chinese who murdered John McDaniels, the town's race track owner, in 1878. The hanging did not take place until March 14, 1879. Sheriff Hank L. McCoy stands on the right of Ah Ben, and Deputy Ike N. Aldrich is on the left. Courtesy California Room, Yuba County Library, Marysville.

Fourth of July celebration in early 1900s, on D Street in Marysville. The people of Marysville loved celebrations. The first California State Fair took place in the community park at Cortez Square in 1853, followed by several more fairs at that location. Currently the Yuba County Court House stands in the square that was once a gathering place for merry-makers. Courtesy California Room, Yuba County Library, Marysville.

Marysville's town orchestra, undated. Seated are William McRae, Amos Brannan, Billy McAdams (owner of the original Owl Saloon) and unknown. Back row left to right are George Herzog (Justice of the Peace and owner of a cigar store) Louis Miller (owner of a saloon on C St.), Arthur McRae, and Ed Bennett. It is thought that they played at the pavilion in Cortez Square. Courtesy California Room, Yuba County Library, Marysville.

Chinese New Year's celebration and Dragon Parade in downtown Marysville, 1880s. Courtesy California Room, Yuba County Library, Marysville.

MANY OF THE Chinese who came to California settled in Marysville, where they established businesses and provided places for entertainment and rest for the gold miners and Chinese laborers. They built a temple to worship several of their gods. Marysville's Bok Kai Temple is the only known temple in the United States honoring Bok Eye. The temple is more accurately known as the Bok Kai Mui, meaning "North (Bok) Temple (Mui) side of the stream (Kai)." Bok Eye, the central Deity in the temple, is honored annually on his birthday (close to the Chinese New Year) with the Bok Kai Festival. For 110 years Bok Eye, the god of water, protected their Bomb Day Parade from being interrupted by rain. However in 1991, when California was suffering from the effects of a five-year drought, Bok Eye showed his power and wisdom by allowing rain to drench the traditional parade. The name "Bomb Day" has been given to the parade as a tribute to Bok Eye because the event features colorful bomb fireworks. It is believed that the Bomb Day celebrations began in 1880 when the present temple was built, although the date may be even earlier.

In 1850, there were 4,025 Chinese residing in the United States. By 1860 Yuba County recorded a Chinese population of 1,781. From sunrise to sunset most Chinese immigrants worked hard and honorably at menial jobs, yet they were often held in contempt, and had few legal or social rights. They were often referred to as "coolies," in Chinese meaning "bitter strength."

Young Chinese girl of Yuba County holding a Marysville penant, circa 1906. Courtesy California Room, Yuba County Library, Marysville.

The annual outing of the Yuba-Sutter Gun Club at Sheldon's Grove, July 31, 1898. Billy Ward, with whiskers, is third from left. Mr. Erwin, fourth from left. Martin Sullivan holding spoon, third from the right. A.C. Bingham, far right, is next to his brother-in-law, W.T. Ellis Jr., who donated land to the city for Ellis Lake, and helped to develop the levee system to protect the town from flooding.
Courtesy California Room, Yuba County Library, Marysville.

THE LATE 1800s brought prosperous days to Marysville. Civic pride was strong. Business was booming, and schools were well established. Marysville would not be one of those towns that faded away after the gold rush was over.

Marysville Grammar School play yard on F Street between 6th and 7th Streets, circa 1915. Courtesy California Room, Yuba County Library, Marysville.

Marysville Post Office under construction, looking west from 4th Street, April 1933. K.E. Parker Co. was the contractor. The earth-moving equipment is still very simple: shovels and muscle. Courtesy Marysville Post Office.

Marysville Post Office, built in 1934, now appears on the Historical Landmark Registry. It is located at 407 C Street in downtown Marysville, across the street from the historic Packard Library building. Currently the Post Office serves the entire 959 zip code area. Courtesy California Room, Yuba County Library, Marysville.

Nurses pose with bed pans at the ready at the old Rideout Hospital, located on 5th Street near E Street, circa 1900. The original Rideout Hospital was situated where the old two-story brick Marysville Hotel now stands.

The old Rideout Hospital, circa 1911. After the death of Norman Dunning Rideout, a prominent banker, in 1907, his wife donated their home on the corner of E and 5th Streets to be used as a hospital. When it was scheduled for removal in 1919 to make way for the Marysville Hotel, Mrs. Rideout donated the land on which today's Rideout Hospital stands. Both photos courtesy Mary Aaron Museum, Marysville.

HAMMONTON

DREDGERS REPLACED hydraulic mining after legislation halted the dumping of debris in the rivers. River bottoms were dredged and sifted to remove the gold that had escaped earlier mining methods. In Hammonton, the Yuba Consolidated Goldfields installed the heaviest known dredger machine used in the industry, capable of digging some 124 feet below water level. Dredgers have again begun their search for gold in the nearby areas that were worked so many years ago.

Hammonton, founded by Wendell Hammon, was a thriving company town from 1906 until 1957, when the town and dredging operations were closed. The houses were sold to their residents for a token price of $1.00, and many of the structures were moved to neighboring communities such as Olivehurst, Linda and Smartville. Today Hammonton exists only in the memories of some local families. Many of Hammonton's residents and their children still live in nearby communities.

Dredger at Hammonton. Courtesy California Room, Yuba County Library, Marysville.

Hammonton Dredger Crew. Fifth person from left top row is Mark Summers, and sixth person Jake ?. Bottom row left to right: ? Jenkins, Ed Bancroft; fifth person is Ira Briggs. Courtesy California Room, Yuba County Library, Marysville.

MARYSVILLE RESOURCES

POINTS OF INTEREST
Ellis Lake - Picnicking, paddle boats, fishing, jogging, duck feeding and relaxing
Mary Aaron Memorial Museum - 704 D Street, (916) 743-1004
Self Guided Tours of Historic Marysville- Maps available at Museum and Chamber of Commerce
Bok Kai Temple- D and 1st Streets,- tours by arrangements
Museum of The Forgotton Warriors - 5865 A Street, (916) 742-3090
Yuba College - North Beale Road.
Silver Dollar Saloon - Corner of D and 1st Streets, (916) 742-9020

SHOPPING & PRODUCE
Marysville Farmers Market - Second Street, late spring and summer months on Wednesday
The Prune Tree - 11289 Highway 70 (Oroville Hwy), (916) 743-5725 nuts, fruit & gift packs
Lomaugh Cherry Orchard - 3095 Walnut Avenue, (916) 743-5793 Fruit May-October
Spring Valley Produce Stand -8 miles east on Highway 20
Chase National Kiwi Farms - 10204 A Highway 70, (916) 743-6422 picnic area
L-M Ranch - 3511 Kibble Road, (916) 743-1314, rice and gift packs
Sodaro Orchards - 9336 Oroville Highway or Highway 70, (916) 743-7735 peaches
Valley Harvest- P.O. Box 2511, (916) 743-1393, rice & gift packs
B. Charles Lemblke Ranch - (916) 743-4535 peaches
Thompson Packing Co.- 10342 Highway 70, (916) 743-7102 or 0480a
Nunes Ranch - 7039 Brophy Road, (916) 741-0355 or 743-5669, freestone peaches, nectarines

FESTIVALS
Bok Kai Festival (Chinese Bomb Day) - Early March on weekend
Beckwourth Western Days (A living museum) - First weekend in October Riverfront Park (916) 743-6501
Flying U Stampede Rodeo- Last weekend in May
Scottish Highland Festival - Third Saturday in May at Riverfront Park
Lion's Wild Hog Glory Daze (Loma Rica) - First Saturday in May
Japanese Obon Festival - Mid July
Greek Food Festival - November
Wear and Rememberance Vintage Apparel Fair - (916) 741-7141

CAMPGROUNDS
Englebright Lake - (916) 634-2342
Camp Far West Reservoir - (916) 645-8069, outside Marysville, near Wheatland
Riverfront Park - Bizz Johnson Drive, (916) 741-6666
Call Yuba Sutter Chamber of Commerce for updated schedules and materials.

The old Yuba County Hospital, circa 1880, located at J and 15th Streets. Part
of the building was still in use in 1940s, but no longer remains.
Courtesy of the Community Memorial Museum, Yuba City.

BEALE AIR FORCE BASE

THE ROLLING FOOTHILLS outside Marysville became a government army camp during WWII. The base was constructed in 1941 and served not only as a training facility, but also as a German Prisoners of War encampment. Named for General Edward F. Beale, a California pioneer and founder of the U.S. Camel Corps, the camp was designated as a U. S. Air Force Base in 1951 and became the home of the now-retired SR-71, the "Blackbird" reconnaissance plane, which set records for altitude, speed, and distance. Beale is also one of four installations in the U.S. of PAVE PAWS, a ten-story radar system that detects sea-launched ballistic missiles. Today Beale Air Force Base is home to 6,912 military personnel and their families.

Above: The U-2 flying over the Golden Gate Bridge in San Francisco. The U-2 is a single-seat, single-engine reconnaissance plane with long, wide and straight wings that give it a glider-like appearance. It flies at speeds up to 450 miles per hour, at an altitude of 70,000 feet. Data collected by this plane not only provide the military with crucial information, but also contribute valuable information about radioactive debris in the stratosphere. An official United States Air Force photograph, courtesy Beale Air Force Base.

Left: Lt. Edward F. Beale, later commissioned Superintendent of Indian Affairs for California and Nevada, 1851. Beale began his military career in the navy and ended it in the army as a brigadier general. He helped to bring the Indian conflicts to an end in California and was one of the few Americans to advocate humane treatment for Indians. Courtesy California Room, Yuba County Library, Marysville.

BEALE RESOURCES
Beale Public Affairs - (916) 634-2137
Edward F. Beale Museum (916) 634-2034
Pow Cell Block - on base
Beale Guest Day - (916) 634-2137 usually held in November

OLIVEHURST

ERLE DISTRICT was a scantily populated open area adjacent to Marysville, south of the Yuba River. A man named Clive Bull, arriving in 1890, had a vision for this land. He bought 20,000 acres, and reclaimed it by building private levees and drainage ditches. In time he plotted out homesites of one acre each in what came to called the "Bull Tract". During the 1930s "Dust Bowl" days, migrant farmers came to California to follow the crops. Along with the displaced mid-western farmers and the relocated Hammonton residents, many local families decided to make these open lands their home. The new community later became known as Olivehurst.

Olivehurst, with a population of 11,191, has endured frequent hardships from flooding, economic stress and slow commercial growth, but the proud citizens have always pulled together and managed to survive.

Men and equipment stacking and baling hay at Erle District.
Courtesy California Room, Yuba County Library, Marysville.

Below: On February 20, 1986, the Yuba River broke through its levee, spilling the raging water through Olivehurst and neighboring Linda. Some 24,000 terrified residents were evacuated with only a few minutes' warning. Water covered some 30 square miles.
Courtesy California Room, Yuba County Library, Marysville.

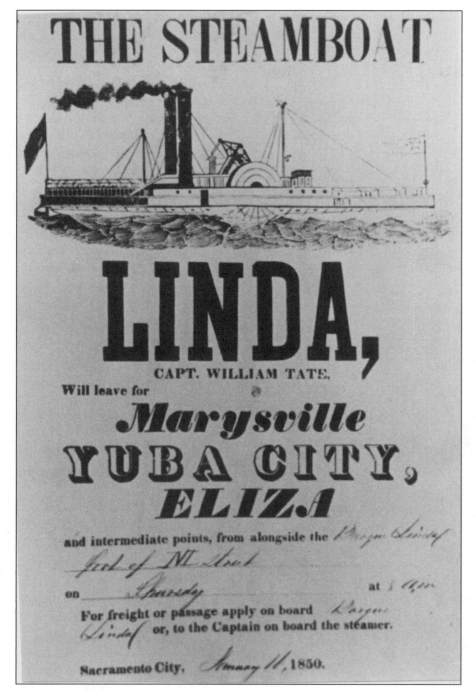

LINDA

LINDA, across the Yuba River from Marysville, was named after the first little steamer that made its way up the Feather and Yuba Rivers. The Linda Company began building up a little town at the anchorage, north of the present Peach Tree Country Club buildings. Originally the area was laid out in 1849 and was called Eliza, but it was soon abandoned when Marysville began to grow rapidly. Now, 140 years later, with the local Junior College situated in the unincorporated town and Beale Air Force Base nearby, new growth has brought the population to a reported 13,033.

The attractive rivers and green valleys of Northern California were a welcome relief to travelers from the "Dust Bowl." Many immigrant workers and their families eventually bought land and settled in the Linda and Olivehurst area.

Billboard ad for the Linda steamer, 1850. Courtesy California Room, Yuba County Library, Marysville.

YUBA CITY

In 1841 German-Swiss John A. Sutter was awarded the Mexican land grant he called New Helvetia, which took in a large portion of the lower Sacramento Valley and extended eastward into the foothills. Later a friend of his, John Bidwell, was sent to manage his Hock Farm, north of New Helvetia, with its Indian rancheria, cattle, orchards and gardens. ("Hock" is believed to come from the German word, "*hoch*," meaning "upper").

In the spring of 1849, Sam Brannan and Pierson B. Reading agreed to pay John Sutter $2,000 for a parcel of land and mapped out a town they hoped would be another booming center. Yuba City, whose name, like Yuba County's, was taken either from wild grapes or a tribe of Maidu Indians, lies across the Feather River from its twin city of Marysville. For a time the two cities were like Siamese twins: what happened in one town immediately affected the other. Being on the side of the river that led to the gold

diggings gave Marysville an advantage. For a long time Yuba City competed with its twin neighbor, but eventually it began to take a different turn. Yuba City flourished as a market town for a great variety of agricultural products. Today the town has few reminders of its early days; it is a fast-growing industrial, commercial and agricultural community of 39,131, surpassing in population its river neighbor. A large variety of fruits, vegetables, grains and nuts are abundant in this area, attracting travelers who like fresh produce.

Construction of the covered bridge, built in 1861 over the Feather River between Marysville and Yuba City. The picture shows the astonishing technological capabilities of the early residents, who must have learned their skills through experience. The bridge served travelers for 46 years before it was destroyed in a 1907 flood. Before it was built, a ferry, operated by George Majors Hanson, crossed the river between the twin towns.
Courtesy Community Memorial Museum, Yuba City.

Bridge Street, circa 1900. Courtesy Community Memorial Museum, Yuba City.

The First National Bank, which later became the Bank of America, on Bridge Street, circa 1890.
Courtesy Community Memorial Museum, Yuba City.

Peach orchard near Yuba City, 1915-1920.
Courtesy California Room, Yuba County Library,
Marysville.

THE YUBA-SUTTER area was once called the Peach Capitol of the World. Over the last several decades, when oversupplies have flooded the markets, many farmers turned to growing prunes. The prune was not only the easiest fruit to preserve, it also provided Americans with fruit during the long winter and spring months, when other fruits were out of season. The French prune, introduced to California in 1856, is a hardy, high-yielding crop, and has made Yuba City the Prune Capitol of the World. The Annual Prune Festival attracts thousands of visitors.

Opposite: Two formidable lawmen,
Yuba County Sheriff Hank McCoy, on
the left, and Sutter County Sheriff
William Harkey, posed for this picture
in 1880. Courtesy California Room,
Yuba County Library, Marysville.

The Yuba City Creamery, circa 1910. Courtesy Special Collections, Meriam Library,
California State University, Chico. (SC 11449)

BEARDED SIKHS with colorful turbans, from the province of Punjab in India, began arriving in the Sacramento Valley early in this century. Unhappy under British rule, many East Indians came to Canada and the United States. Between 1906 and 1910 large numbers of Sikhs came to the Sacramento Valley to find work laying roadbeds for the Western Pacific and the Northern Electric Railroads. Some returned to their homeland when the work was completed, but others stayed.

Kartar Singh is thought to be the first East Indian to purchase land in Sutter County in 1913 before the enactment of the Alien Land Law. In the early 1920s the new law prevented the purchase of land by any alien not married to an American citizen. During WW II, Balwant Singh Sidhu, a Sutter resident, was the first East Indian alien to be drafted into the United States military. By 1959 Sutter County had become the largest East Indian (Sikh and Hindu) community in the United States. When citizenship was given to military veterans of alien status, many of these families, who were known for their farming skills, purchased peach and prune orchards.

The County Courthouse (left) was built in the Greek Revival style in 1899, and the Sutter County Hall of Records, (right) in Romanesque style, in 1891. Both buildings are still in use at their original location on Second Street. Yuba City became the county seat for Sutter County in 1856. Courtesy Sutter County Library, Yuba City.

Yuba City Grammar School, circa 1915. The quality of the design and construction reflect the high value placed on education in the early years of this century. Courtesy California Room, Yuba County Library, Marysville.

The Harkey House, at 212 C Street, was built in 1874. Sheriff William (Bill) Harkey, a former grain farmer in Yuba County, built this fine home near his work at the Sutter County Courthouse. The Harkey House now is open to the public as a lovely bed and breakfast inn and a reception hall.

Many Yuba City area residents remember the flood of Christmas Eve, 1955, shown looking north on Plumas Street. Marysville residents, fearful of the rising Yuba River, had earlier been evacuated to Yuba City, the unsuspecting sleeping town that was thought to be safe. The levee system, constructed to contain the raging Feather River, broke on Christmas Eve, south of Yuba City at Shanghai Bend. Thirty-eight people lost their lives, with an estimated $81 million in damage. Today it is a costly and constant undertaking to monitor and maintain the levee systems, owned by various state, county, and local governments and several water districts.
Courtesy Sutter County Library, Yuba City.

The 5th Street Bridge, washed out by the swift-running Feather River during the 1955 flood.
Courtesy Sutter County Library, Yuba City.

YUBA CITY RESOURCES

POINTS OF INTEREST
Community Memorial Museum of Sutter Country - 1333 Butte House Road, (916) 741-7141
Memorial Park - A tribute to WW I soldiers, a path at the head of Bridge Street with a stairway to top of levee
Sikh Temple - 2468 Tierra Buena Road, built in 1970, (916) 671-9853 or 673-8623, Temple at 2465 Bogue Road.
John Sutter's Hock Farm - The historic site is off Highway 99, (Garden Highway)
Self Guided Tours of Historic Yuba City - Maps available at Museum or Chamber of Commerce in Marysville
Harter House - A private home, built in 1872, on Harter Road across the entrance to Harter's Cannery
Teegarden House - A private home, built in 1880 on 731 Plumas Street
Bogue House - A private home, built in the 1880s on 712 Bogue Road

FESTIVALS
California Prune Festival - Second weekend in September at the Yuba Sutter Fairgrounds
Yuba Sutter County Fair - End of July at the fairgrounds

SHOPPING & PRODUCE
Yuba City Farmer's Market - Center Street, off Plumas Street - Summer months on Saturday mornings
Sunsweet Grower's Store - 901 N. Walton Avenue, (916) 674-5010, dried fruit, nuts & gift packs
Johnson's Farm - 6255 Highway 99, fruit, vegetables, nuts, pies, jams and breads
Deer Creek Wild Rice - 785 Sutter Street, (916) 671-6649
Taylor Fruit & Juice Co..- 1320 O'Banion Road, (916) 671-4400
Sally Broce - 3637 Lincoln Road, (916) 674-2426, organic, mail order
The Orchid Obsession - 1477 Oswald Road,
 (916) 673-2114, orchids (January - July)
Don Perrin's Pecans - 27 CYPRESS Avenue,
 (916) 674-0177, nuts, pears, apples

BED AND BREAKFAST INNS
Harkey House Bed and Breakfast - 212 C Street,
 (916) 674-1942
Moore's Mansion Inn - Corner Bridge Street
 and Cooper Avenue, (916) 674-7951

*John A. Sutter. Courtesy
California Room, Yuba
County Library, Marysville.*

SUTTER

SUTTER, a small rural community, lies at the base of the picturesque Sutter Buttes. The unincorporated settlement, surrounded by hills, waterways, and grain fields, is nine miles west of Yuba City. Sutter, like nearby communities, attracts fowl hunters during the fall, and fishermen in spring and summer months.

The Sutter Buttes, alleged to be the "Smallest Range of Mountains in the World" and formed about 2½ million years ago, are a landmark for travelers and a pleasing bit of scenery for Sutter County residents. They have been visited by such historic people as Gabriel Moraga, Jedediah Smith, Hudson Bay Company trappers, and John C. Fremont. In years gone by, Maidu Indian villages were located among the rolling oak-studded terrain. The rocky slopes have yielded a little gold, a coal vein, and stone from several quarries. Today the Buttes not only provide sand and gravel for builders and natural gas for energy, they also are a unique recreation area for bicyclists, joggers and sightseers. Andesite boulders are scattered throughout the hillsides of the Buttes as a reminder of a volcanic explosion over 1.35 million years ago. Many of the fields have rock fences, piled and stacked by Chinese laborers and farmers in order to prepare the land for farming and to serve as boundary lines.

Today's Sutter Buttes, originally called Marysville Buttes. The native Maidu Indians called them "Histum Yani" meaning "Middle Mountains of the Valley." Courtesy California Room, Yuba County Library, Marysville.

IN 1884 Peter D. Gardemeyer, a sewing machine salesman, arrived in the small hamlet of Sutter. He married a local rancher's widow, Mrs. Herman Erke, and appointed himself Sutter's land developer. His grand idea was to hold a sale and lottery for 300 building lots from a parcel purchased from George Summy. The grand prize was to be a lot with a hotel. There was even a plan for the little community to have a college to compete with College of the Pacific in Stockton. The promise of Sutter as a boom town and county government center never materialized. But the little settlement did survive and flourish in a modest way. It is now home to 3,000 residents.

To impress the townspeople Gardemeyer built a beautiful brick mansion for his wife. But when accusations about his character and financial dealings began to surface, he left hurriedly for Texas. Some years later the house burned, and his estranged wife was murdered by Peter Schmitt, a German immigrant who had been left destitute by Gardemeyer's promises and grand promotions.

Peter D. Gardemeyer

The Gardemeyer mansion. Both photos courtesy of the Community Memorial Museum, Yuba City.

California Street in Sutter, circa 1900. In the foreground is the Felts Building (Sutter Hotel and old Post Office), built in 1890. The building in the background, at California and Nelson Streets, was built in 1889 as a bank, yet was never used for that purpose. For decades it housed the Native Daughters of the Golden West. Today it stands, in much need of repair. Courtesy Community Memorial Museum, Yuba City.

Sutter Hotel, circa 1900. The hotel also housed a store and the Post Office. Today the Sutter Post Office stands on the site and still uses the original well. Courtesy Meriam Library, California State University, Chico, Special Collections. (SC 9840)

The first women's basketball team at Sutter High School, circa 1905. Back row from left are Maude King, Mr. Rathbun, Ellea Wilson. In the center is the ball girl, Elva Talmadge. Front row from left are Neta Davis, Ora Percy (Epperson) and Hazel Moore. Courtesy Marc Ockerman.

Sutter High School bus, 1920s. Courtesy Otto Becker.

The splendid Sutter High School on South Butte Road was built in 1894. Courtesy Community Memorial Museum, Yuba City.

EDWIN THURMAN became the first white settler in the Sutter Buttes when he built his cabin in 1851. He raised cattle near Pass Road, a stage route from Marysville to Colusa. In 1853, George Brittan took over the Thurman ranch and built a fine stone house for his family. Brittan Elementary School is named for George Brittan, who is thought of as the first permanent resident in the town of Sutter.

Other early settlers include Herman Utt, Golder DeWitt, the Tarke family and the Getty family. These Sutter pioneers helped to clear oak trees from the land to prepare it for raising grain, almonds, rice and other valuable crops.

George Brittan took seven years to build this house on Pass Road from stone quarried in the Sutter Buttes. Later bought by Clarence DeWitt, the 1859 house is now owned by the Willard LeBaron family. Courtesy Community Memorial Museum, Yuba City.

A MONUMENT stands today at the spot where General John C. Fremont camped along Pass Road, among the rolling hills of the Sutter Buttes in 1846, when California belonged to Mexico. His purpose was to rally local American settlers, as well as to assure them of protection against possible Indian attacks. At the campsite, plans were discussed that led to the Bear Flag Revolt and the American conquest of California.

*The John C. Fremont Historical Monument.
Courtesy Otto Becker, photographer.*

*John C. Fremont. Courtesy California Room,
Yuba County Library, Marysville.*

SUTTER RESOURCES

POINTS OF INTEREST

Fremont Monument - Pass Road
B. Thompson Seedless Grapes Historic Marker- Highway 20
Brittan House - A private home, built in 1869 on Pass Road
Henry S. Graves House - A private home, built in 1870 on West
Butte Road
Frederick Tarke House - A private home, built in 1885 on West
Butte Road
Sutter Buttes - Oil wells, rock fences, historic cemeteries, aban
doned missile base site, early townsite of Pennington.

EVENTS

Sutter Buttes Day - First weekend in June
Lions Club Striper Derby - Last weekend in May, a striper
fishing contest with many prizes
**Rural Artisans' Old Fashioned Christmas Happening and
Pheasant Hunters Breakfast** - Second weekend in November
Bike Around The Buttes - First Saturday in April,
(916) 674-9112

SHOPPING

McPherrin's Sheep Skins - (916) 755-0077

Off for the Picnic, Colusa, Cal.

Captain Gabriel Moraga, on one of his expeditions upstream from San Francisco Bay, explored the river that sprang from streams near Mt. Shasta and flowed for 382 miles to the ocean. In 1808, having reached a point some 25 miles north of present-day Meridian, he decided to call this massive river "Rio del Sacramento." Here a steamboat loads passengers for a picnic up river at Grimes. As many as 1,000 people would attend the annual picnic. Courtesy Sacramento Valley Museum, Williams.

SACRAMENTO RIVER TOWNS

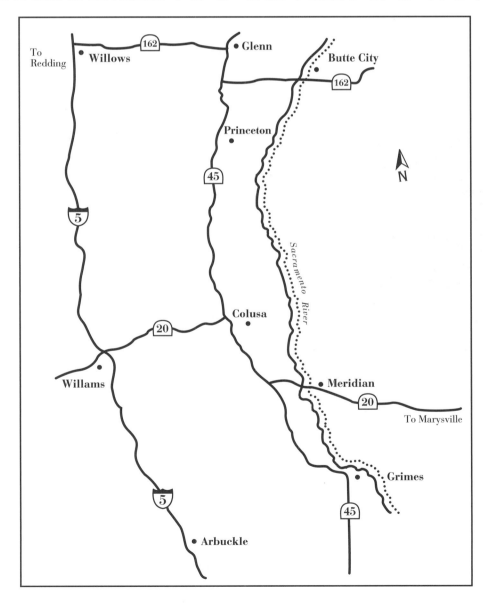

MERIDIAN

MERIDIAN, a farm town west of Marysville with 1,030 residents, sits on the banks of the Sacramento River, and affords great fishing spots with convenient boat landings and docking facilities. The town's history has always been connected to the renowned waterway.

Back in 1860, John F. Fouts established a much-needed ferry for crossing the troublesome river. The small settlement that grew up came to known as Fouts' Ferry, but later was called Meridian, because it was only a quarter mile from the meridian line of the U.S. Survey of California from Mt. Diablo baseline through the Sacramento Valley. The first bridge built to replace the ferry was erected in 1913, opening the west side of the valley to more convenient traveling.

Losey's Department Store. Courtesy Community Memorial Museum, Yuba City.

Meridian Ferry, circa 1900; the man at the rail is E.B. Jacobs. Courtesy Community Memorial Museum, Yuba City.

MERIDIAN RESOURCES

Lovey's Landing - On the river, campground, boat-launch and home-cooking cafe. (916) 695-2449
The Paine House - A remodeled private home built in 1872 on the corner of Meridian and Maroni Roads

---

Meridian Wednesday Embroidery Club at the Meridian Hotel, circa 1912. Mrs. Boyd Taylor was the proprietor of the hotel. Shown from left are Irma Taylor, unknown, Alice Reische, Rose Wheeler, Sarah Strode Rockholt, Mrs. Boyd Taylor, unknown, Bessie Gramier Jones, Ethel Jones Albertson, unknown, Tellie Meier, Bessie Thompson, Hannah Jacobs, unknown, Mamie Shannon Smith, Mrs. Bodie Taylor, the child is Dallas Smith Sprigg.
Courtesy Sutter County Museum, Yuba City and Meriam Library, California State University, Chico. (SC 9838)

Slough School, near the Long Bridge, circa 1890. Today the school still stands near Tarke Warehouse, but is not being used. Courtesy Community Memorial Museum, Yuba City.

GRIMES

GRIMES, with 605 residents, nestles against the west bank of the Sacramento River, south of Meridian. The town's founder was Cleaton Grimes. In early days Grimes was a shipping port for the large grain exports grown in the northern Sacramento Valley. Today people in pleasure boats cruise the river in search of fish, enjoying views of the farm lands, grain mills, and the picturesque Sutter Buttes, not much different from 150 years ago.

In the early 1900s wild geese came in such vast numbers that they caused enormous damage to valuable grain crops. The geese not only ate their weight in precious grain, they would trample down the fields while feeding. "Geese Herders" were hired to ride their horses at night, shooting or scaring away the pests to help protect the crops. Ducks also were so abundant that hunters were constantly encouraged to come and get their limits. Around 1914 they say that in one night ducks ate some 640 acres of rice and whole fields of alfalfa and clover. During the Depression years, a man told how he had gathered ducks along the roadside to take to San Francisco and sold them to the Mark Hopkins Hotel, receiving $1,000 for his small efforts. Grimes today still offers great hunting opportunities in autumn, when grain crops are harvested and the migrating flocks arrive.

In the winter of 1861-62 a great flood covered the entire Sacramento Valley, with some 37 inches of rainfall recorded that season. When the land was unable to drain naturally, pumps were used to rid the land of the unwanted standing water. At one time Grimes had the world's largest pump, which was able not only to pump out the flooded areas, but to reverse its mechanics and pump water back for irrigation later.

Hunters display their trophies. Both photos courtesy Sacramento Valley Museum, Williams.

Rice sacks ready for shipping down river.

Above and below: Threshing rice with threshing machines driven by huge steam-powered tractors. circa 1930. Courtesy Special Collections, Meriam Library, California State University, Chico. (SC 11670)

Photo courtesy Sacramento Valley Museum, Williams.

Above: Grimes Branch, Colusa County Bank, undated. This historic building, designed as a Greek temple to hold the fortunes of wheat and rice farmers, today stands empty. Courtesy Sacramento Valley Museum, Williams, and Meriam Library, California State University, Chico, Special Collection. (SC 1161)

Right: Sycamore Church, near Grimes, was organized in 1875 and built at a cost of $4,000. Sycamore, once a thriving spot in Colusa County, still stirs strong memories among local historians and old-timers. Today a historic brick Catholic shrine stands at Sycamore: a miniature house of worship, built in 1883 on the site where the first Catholic Mass was held in Colusa County by Father Walrath, missionary to local Indians. The tiny shrine is hardly bigger than a backyard tool shed. Courtesy Meriam Library, California State University, Chico, Special Collections. (SC 10239)

GRIMES RESOURCES

Miniature Catholic Shrine - (Ripley's World's Smallest Church) - near Sycamore on Highway 45
Davis Ranch House - private three-story brick house built in 1892 near Sycamore
Old Grimes Bank - Main Street in Grimes

COLUSA

Colusa, 65 miles northwest of Sacramento, the county seat of Colusa County, the leading rice producing county in the United States, has a population of 4,934. The neighboring coastal range and the Sacramento River form the boundaries of the rural community, which is a mecca for avid hunters and fishermen. Several wildlife reserves in the area allow naturalists to study the migration of ducks, geese and other birds. The northern Sacramento River country is the prime area of the Pacific flyway, where waterfowl come during the winter season. Three National Wildlife Refuges are in Colusa County.

Colusa County Courthouse, built in 1861, is the oldest courthouse remaining in the Sacramento Valley. The bell and tower were added to the building in 1886. The movie "To Kill A Mockingbird", starring Gregory Peck, was filmed at this location. Courtesy Sacramento Valley Museum, Williams.

A fine Queen Anne style residence in Colusa. The town has long been known for beautiful Victorian houses built in the late 1800s, and for well-kept historic churches standing along lovely shaded streets. It is a conservative community, rich in buildings and traditions worth conserving. Courtesy Sacramento Valley Museum, Williams.

COLUSA WAS first known as Colusi (or Corusi), named for the Coru Indian tribe residing in the area. They were a hunting, fishing and gathering tribe whose lives evolved around the Sacramento River. When the white man came to the area, the tribe numbered approximately 1,000, but within a few years the population had almost vanished. The Indian Chief Sioc was remembered for his kindness and good relations with new homesteaders. Today Colusa has a street named in his honor. Land along the Sacramento River has been set aside for resident native Americans.

In years past, the valley was mostly swampland and waterways, which were later reclaimed by drains and levee systems. Today the area is rich in agricultural abundance and modern farming technology. Because of limited rainfall and the need of many crops for large volumes of water, Colusa and neighboring counties developed very efficient irrigation systems, among the finest in the nation.

*Colusa's first school, circa 1858.
Courtesy Sacramento
Valley Museum, Williams.*

*Hotel Riverside in 1895. Courtesy Meriam library, California State University,
Chico, Special Collections. (SC 8686)*

In 1892, the automobile was invented, and by 1907 there were 27 cars in Colusa County. Colusa's first auto race and parade took place in 1909. Courtesy Willows Museum and Meriam Library, California State University, Special Collections. (SC 13652)

Colusa County was referred to as the "South Carolina of California" during the Civil War. Some county officials were held in the military prison on Alcatraz for voicing Southern sympathies too loudly. In more recent times, politics calmed down; I.G. Zumwalt ran for congress in 1910, but was defeated. Courtesy Sacramento Valley Museum, Williams.

An outing in Colusa County, circa 1900. Courtesy Sacramento Valley Museum, Williams and Special Collections, Meriam Library, California State University, Chico. (SC 12103)

COLUSA RESOURCES

POINTS OF INTEREST
Historic Colusa County Courthouse - Market Street, downtown Colusa
Historic Chinatown - Main Street, downtown Colusa
Wintun Indian Bingo -Highway 45, toll-free 1-800-225-8393
Colusa - Sacramento State Park - Off Main Street
Colusa Nation Wildlife Refuge - Highway 45
Sacramento National Wildlife Refuge - Interstate 5
Delevan Wildlife Reserve - Off Maxwell Road and Interstate 5
Colusa Chamber Of Commerce - (916) 458-2541
The Little Catholic Shrine- "Smallest Church in the World", off Highway 20 between Meridian and Colusa

EVENTS
Colusa Farm Show - First weekend in February
Colusa County Fair - Third weekend in June at the fairgrounds in Colusa
Colusa Waterfowl and Rice Festival -First weekend in November. Call (916) 458-2541 for details

BED AND BREAKFAST INNS
O'Rourke's Mansion - 1765 Lurline Avenue, (916) 458-5625

CAMPGROUNDS
High Street Trailer Park - (916) 458-4424
Cruise 'N Tarry Marina Trailer Park - (916) 458-2617
Colusa - Sacramento River State Park and Recreation Area - (916) 458-4927
Emerald Cove Resort & Marina - (916) 692-2166

PRINCETON

PRINCETON, a pretty little town on the banks of the Sacramento River, 17 miles north of Colusa on Highway 45, is one of the three oldest settlements in Colusa County. Like Grimes and Colusa, it was a shipping port for locally grown crops. Princeton is probably best known for its historic ferry. The ferry still operates 24 hours a day across the Sacramento River, and has been recorded in Ripley's "Believe it or Not." The ferry has survived many hardships to remain operational since the 1850s. Of the 39 ferries that have transported cargo and passengers across the Sacramento River, the Princeton Ferry is the only one still running today.

For many years Colusa was referred to as the "Cow County". The countryside was known for its immense cattle herds. Princeton was a center for the cattle business as well as multi-grain crops. Today it is quite small in comparison to most valley communities, but it is a memorable town with its mixture of old and new buildings, and a long tradition of citizens working hand in hand, binding together the large and small farmers and their beloved home town.

In 1847 John S. Williams built the first house in Colusa County on the banks of the Sacramento River near the present site of Princeton. Thomas O. Larkin, only U.S. Consul to California under the Mexican rule, sent Williams to the area to start up a cattle ranch in the name of his children. The prosperous 1,000- acre cattle ranch was known and still is referred to as the Larkin Children's Grant.

The Princeton Ferry of today. Phil Shepherd, photographer.

"Cow Country". Courtesy Sacramento Valley Museum Williams.

Julius Loeb's General Merchandise store in Princeton, circa 1912. It is believed that part of this building is still standing. Courtesy of Meriam Library, California State University, Chico, Special Collections. (SC 12014)

Princeton Hotel, circa 1912. The date of construction is much earlier. Courtesy of the Meriam Library, California State University, Chico, Special Collections. (SC 12013)

Glenn Post Office and Store in earlier days. Courtesy Willows Museum and Meriam Library, California State University, Chico, Special Collections. (SC 13646)

APPROXIMATELY 27 miles north of Colusa was Dr. Hugh Glenn's business farm, known as Jacinto Village. The village supported a general store, a post office, a hotel, several blacksmith shops, a butcher shop, several grain houses and a shipping dock. Today Jacinto Village only exists in the historic records.

Presently Glenn has 928 residents. The surrounding areas of Glenn County have long been a gathering place for a large and prominent population of Mennonites, who brought to the valley their peaceable attitudes, as well as highly evolved farming techniques and business acumen, contributing a strong economic backbone to the community.

BUTTE

BUTTE CITY, population 525, on the east bank of the Sacramento River, is a very small place, but the surrounding farms are abundantly planted with grains, nuts and vegetables. Steamboats stopped at the Butte City Landing or passed under this bridge for many years, hauling lumber from counties farther north. The banks of the river were so overgrown with trees and vines that boats could not make their way through the thicket, and could dock only at developed landings. Over the years the brush was thinned to allow more access to the surrounding land. Today the California Department of Fish and Game is purchasing land along the river and letting the banks return to the original natural state, not only to aid in the fish runs, but also to re-establish lost wetlands.

The Neponset No. 2, *circa 1910, is seen steaming under the bridge which still stands at Butte City. A closer look reveals a horse and buggy on the bridge. The steamer is unloading supplies at this stop. The stack of wood on the shore is waiting to be shipped downriver. Courtesy Meriam Library, California State University, Chico, Special Collections. (SC 8625)*

THE
HEART
of the
VALLEY

Steam threshing rig at harvest, 1880-1890. Courtesy Sutter County Library, Yuba City.

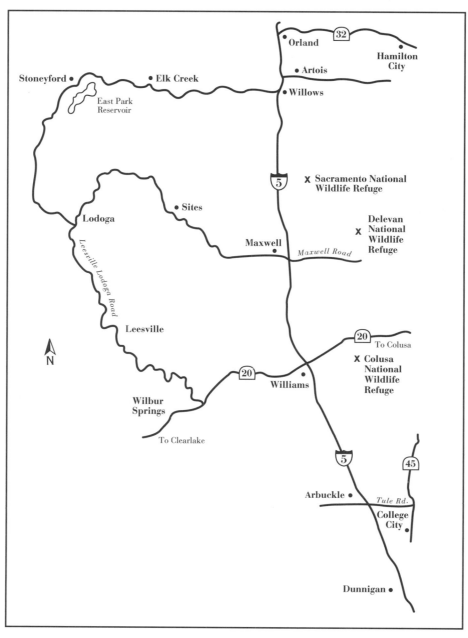

DUNNIGAN

THE FIRST POSTMASTER of this agricultural community, in 1855, was A.W. Dunnigan, a farmer from whom the town takes its name. Along with his partner, H. Yarick, he owned the first hotel and blacksmith shop. Dunnigan, once called Antelope, is the southernmost community presented in this Heartland section, at the edge of Yolo County. J.S. Clapp and John Wilson were the first white settlers to come to the area in 1853. By 1876 the railroad came up through the fertile valley, bring new settlers.

This stretch of land was once home to grizzly bears, elk, deer, antelope, wolves, and beavers. California native tribes thrived on this bounty and outsiders were drawn to it very early. Beaver attracted trappers during the Mexican period. Then came American settlers, who saw this fruitful land as a perfect place to raise crops and families. The Indians soon vanished from their native homeland.

Triumph Church stands near a quaint, narrow bridge on the edge of Dunnigan, circa 1990. Phil Shepherd, photographer.

At Happy Camp, near Dunnigan on the Colusa County border, a hunting party prepares to toot its own horns, circa 1890. Courtesy Sacramento Valley Museum, Williams, and Special Collection, Meriam Library, California State University, Chico. (SC 12995)

ARBUCKLE

IN 1875, when the Northern Railroad worked its way into the middle of the Northern Sacramento Valley, the citizens of College City refused to allow the tracks to be laid through their town. Tacitus R. Arbuckle, owner of about 7,320 acres, saw a golden opportunity to build up another town within 3 miles of College City. He donated much of the land for the new town, which was named for its founder. The new settlement grew as a shipping point for locally grown wheat, barley, rice, almonds and various other products. Today Arbuckle has 1,912 residents and is a growing farming community straddling Interstate 5.

A momentary spotlight fell on the little community when remains of a prehistoric pig were found 50 feet underground near Cortina Creek in 1952. Along with the previous discovery of a prehistoric skeletal fossil in Live Oak, the rare discovery provided geologic information about the valley's strata, establishing the age of the Tehama water-bearing formation, which supplies water to irrigation wells. Irrigation has increased the yield of several bean varieties, such as kidneys, limas, blackeyes and pinks.

Land being prepared for the planting of almond trees. Courtesy of Sacramento Valley Museum, Williams.

ARBUCKLE RESOURCES

Circle Produce - (916) 476-3381, strawberries, vegetables and melons, April - October
Irene's Apricot Farm- (916) 473-5418 or 476-2377
Wiggins Farms - (916) 476-2288 or 476-2856 (fax), nuts, beef, hay, fit packs and mail order
Portello Ranch - (916) 756-0842 or 476-2204, nuts, mail order, September - December

Bradford's Blacksmith Shop, Arbuckle, Henry Humphrey, right, and Tony Felton ,left, circa 1925. Courtesy Sacramento Valley Museum, Williams, and California State University, Chico, Special Collection. (SC 10958)

Arbuckle's first auto fire truck, "Ready for Action." When Arbuckle outgrew this truck the town donated it to College City. Courtesy of Sacramento Valley Museum, Williams.

COLLEGE CITY

THE DEVELOPMENT of this area began with two separate colonies settled by Swedes and Germans. College City, with only three businesses on main street, is perched among tomato fields, almond orchards, rice fields and grain fields east of Arbuckle. Today's visitor might be surprised to know that this town of only 835 once really was a college town. Andrew Pierce, a shoemaker, owned a profitable sheep ranch in the vicinity. Upon his death in 1871, the money from the sale of his estate was used to start Pierce Christian College, which opened in 1876, one of the earliest institutions of higher learning in California. In 1897 the college was moved to Southern California, and the building was used as Pierce High School until 1936. By 1945 the well-used school was torn down. A local historian says that today's Los Angeles Pierce College in Southern California is not affiliated with this historic college.

Standing beside the College was a remarkably beautiful church featuring splendid stained-glass windows, gas-lit chandeliers, ornate baptismal doors, a grand wooden pulpit, and a mahogany interior. During a period of its vacancy while efforts were being made to establish it as a historic site, the treasures were stolen, and the beloved old relic was criminally vandalized. Finally the church was destroyed; its sole remaining treasure, the bell, was given a place of honor at College City Cemetery. This tragic loss serves as a painful lesson in preservation.

Pierce Christian College, shown in a painting by Raymond K. Patton. Courtesy of Sacramento Valley Museum, Williams, and Meriam Library, California State University, Chico, Special Collection. (SC 12988)

Pierce Christian College students and faculty, College City, April 1891. A co-educational Christian college was a rarity in this era. The students included many members of Sacramento Valley families, for whom the college was conveniently accessible. A rather confusing legend on the back of the photograph reads as follows: First row: Willard Hale, Arthur Burnett, Herman Yates, John Foster, C.A. Brown, Will Murdock, Lee Jones, Milton Snowball, Will Eddy, John Wylie, Warren White. Second row: Joe ?, George Wallbridge, J.E. ?, Harry Bridgeford, Walter Burnett, Harry Houston, Lee Watson, John King, George Ford, Bert Gibbons, Will White, W.A. Rice, R.A. Logan, A.E. Byers. Third row: Mary Ingram, Etta Moore, Lou Raper, Rose Gregory, Gertie Gillaspy, Hattie Alexander, Alta Lane, Nela Yates, Pearl Keith, Lillian Stewart, Dollie ?, Effie Foster. Fourth row: Ruby Bashore, Alma Eddy, Dell Teaby, Maggie ?, Carrie Miller.
Courtesy Sacramento Valley Museum, Williams, and Meriam Library,
California State University, Chico, Special Collection. (SC 11637)

WILLIAMS

Top: Aerial View of Williams.
Courtesy Sacramento Valley Museum, Williams.

WILLIAMS, with its historic Welcome Arch, sits proudly at the junction of Highway 20 and Interstate 5. The entire area is dotted with grain warehouses and silos to hold the bountiful local harvests. People who like taste tours and sampling farm-fresh wares at roadside stands will find plenty to do in Williams.

The town is named for W.H. Williams, a hotel owner and local farmer of the late 1850s. The arrival of the railroad opened the doors to the development of this community. With the Southern Pacific Railroad running through the center of town and its proximity to Highway 20 and the Interstate 5 crossroads, Williams today is considered to be the transportation hub of Colusa County. With a population of 2,297, the junction city serves as the Northern Sacramento Valley's gateway to the Pacific Coast.

Very early street scene Williams. Courtesy Sacramento Valley Museum, Williams.

A steam-powered tractor attracts plenty of attention in Williams around 1900. The horses, whose days are numbered, seem indifferent. Courtesy Sacramento Valley Museum, Williams, and Special Collection, Meriam Library, California State University, Chico. (SC 10922)

Williams School, circa 1878. Note the signs over the two doors separating the genders. Courtesy Sacramento Valley Museum, Williams.

Built in 1911, Sacramento Valley Museum, originally Williams High School, circa 1991. One of the most interesting exhibits is a massive doll display tracing the history of fashion through 1927. Sandy Shepherd, photographer.

WILLIAMS RESOURCES

Sacramento Valley Museum - 1492 E Street (old Hwy. 20), (916) 473-2978
Pioneer Days - First weekend in June
Leesville Hotel - Leesville, west of Williams. The building was an early day stagecoach stop and hotel. Built in 1878, the hotel today is used as a private home.
Wilbur Hot Springs - Hotel built in 1918. The hot springs and hotel is still open west of Williams off Highway 20 on the Wilbur Hot Springs Road

MAXWELL

MAXWELL, a spread out farming community, sits in the center of the Sacramento Valley and Colusa County. The town was first plotted out as the townsite of Occident, but was later named after George Maxwell, who earned the honor by donating land for the railroad station. As the Northern Railroad neared the townsite, the area grew in population.

Around 1917, Maxwell had the largest lemon orchard in the world; people arrived from all over to work in the citrus harvest. During the "Dust Bowl" days, many families came to the area to find work in these orchards. The Mill Orchard shipped up to a carload of lemons each day, but freezing winters finally led to its closure after smudge pot heating (oil burning in pots and placed in orchards) became too expensive.

Today Maxwell, seems to be a sleepy little back country community with a population of 1,441, but townspeople are restoring some of their older buildings and bringing life back to their doorstep.

A quiet day in Maxwell, around 1900. Courtesy of Bob Nation, Maxwell Postmaster

MAXWELL AREA RESOURCES

Old Opera House - Known as the Legion Hall, built in 1912, used today for town functions.
Brown's Garage- Built in 1910, the first concrete building in the area.
Union Hall- Built in late 1800s
Stone Corral- 6 miles west of Maxwell
Sites Sandstone Quarries- West of Maxwell, two quarries remain where the greyish-blue sandstone was supplied for many well known buildings in San Francisco.
Fouts Spring - West of Stoneyford, once a health spa and now a boys' camp
Maxwell Saloon - Old time western steak house and dance hall on the site of George Maxwell's Pioneer Saloon
Chateau Basque - Unique French and Basque food

The Old Brick Maxwell School, circa 1871: Maxwell's first high school and grammar school. Courtesy Sacramento Valley Museum, Williams.

Maxwell Union Grammar School, circa 1922. The school buses were called "Green Frogs." Neither schoolhouse remains standing. Courtesy Sacramento Valley Museum, Williams.

SITES

SITES, THE GATEWAY from valley to coast range mountains, is now almost a ghost town. It lies amid the rolling hills just west of Maxwell and south of Stoneyford. This grassy glen was once called Antelope Valley; the wild oats stood so thick and tall that antelopes could hide. John Sites, for whom the old town is named, began his cattle enterprise in this little basin. The old resting point for many a traveler was also the source of an important natural building material. The sandstone quarry's operation was started by Alfred Knowles. Stone slabs were cut and carried to the train for hauling to Colusa, then made their way to San Francisco by way of the Sacramento River. Several buildings in San Francisco were built from the quarry, including the St. Frances Hotel, the Flood Building, the old Hall of Justice, the Shreve Building, and the Ferry Building.

The Burrows Stone Corral at Sites, a reminder of the old cattle days, circa 1915. Courtesy Bob Nation.

Sandstone quarry site. For generations visitors have scaled the mountain side to sign their names in the stone. Phil Shepherd, photographer.

The Colusa and Lake train line never went beyond Sites, but it made many trips between Colusa and the depot. Stone from nearby quarries was used to build the San Francisco Emporium as well as the Colusa Library. The little train ran daily, hauling cargo between the two towns, but was loaded with far too much weight for its size, and the engine would sometimes topple over. Despite numerous derailments the train kept on hauling stone out and passengers in to nearby mountain health spas. Leo Burrows and Mark Burrows stand by the train, above. Both photos courtesy Bob Nation.

STONEYFORD

Stoneyford was first named Smithville after the flour mill and hotel owner, John Smith. The town lies among the rolling hills of the coastal range adjacent to the Sacramento Valley. Not many crops are raised in the area, for much of the soil is alkaline. But lush green meadows with babbling streams in the springtime invite an expanding livestock industry. The surrounding area is beginning to see growth as newcomers relocate to this quiet, remote Indian country. Today Stoneyford is home to some 528 residents. Stoneyford may be best noted for its East Park Reservoir, built in 1910. The Reservoir was the first federal reclamation project built in California and is one of the oldest in the U.S.

Mountain House in Colusa County near Stoneyford, where the stagecoach lines stopped for a rest, circa 1893. Mountain House was recently demolished. Courtesy Sacramento Valley Museum, Williams, and Meriam Library, California State University, Chico, Special Collection. (SC 10912)

A pumpkin patch at Haddick's Bar, Stoneyford, circa 1885. Courtesy California State Library, California Section.

STONEYFORD RESOURCES

Stoneyford Rodeo - First weekend
 in May
**East Park Reservoir
Campgrounds** - (916) 963-3141
St. Mary's Catholic Church

ELK CREEK

ELK CREEK is in Glenn County, west of Willows, at the junction of Elk and Stony Creeks. This mountain village, with its weathered wood frame houses and dated buildings, lies among rolling foothills and ancient oaks. The population of this remote area is made up primarily of Native Americans.

Grindstone Dance House, six miles north of Elk Creek, shown in 1949, probably built in 1894. At one time Elk Creek was the center of a very large Indian Reservation, their territory covering some 1.6 million acres. Today the Nomlaki Wintun Indians own only an 80-acre parcel of land below the Black Butte Reservoir. Courtesy Willows Museum.

Early days in Elk Creek. Miller's blacksmith shop and Knight Butler Lucas store are shown, but not identified. Courtesy Meriam Library, California State University, Chico, Special Collection. (SC 87

WILLOWS

WILLOWS, with 5,988 residents, invites visitors to California's Food Basket of the World. The towns in this area overflow with almonds, olives, tomatoes, citrus, beans, rice and much more. Willows is also lamb country. The town is proud of its livestock and its many beautiful farms. Waterfowl and pheasant are plentiful in the golden grain fields, laced with waterways. Today's visitor to Willows, with its wide streets and well kept homes, manicured lawns, and handsome government buildings, may find it hard to imagine that it was once only a waterhole bordered with willow trees, from which it got its name.

Old City Hall, torn down in the early 1970s. Courtesy Willows Museum.

Willows' elegantly symmetrical courthouse in a dream-like mist, circa 1990.
Phil Shepherd, photographer.

60

IN 1852, Nathaniel Bowman was the first person to be found guilty and hanged in Colusa County, later renamed Glenn County. William Brown Ide, the first and only President of California Republic, served as judge, defense attorney, prosecuting attorney, court recorder and jailer on this case.

The moving of the old Willows High School by Charles Roberts, contractor. Courtesy Willows Museum.

The first trial jury in Glenn County in 1891, the year the county was officially established. They convicted J.S. LeRoy of murder and imprisoned him for life. Courtesy Willows Museum.

Above: Willows' "Million Dollar Fire", July 11, 1920. Courtesy Willows Museum and Meriam Library, California State University, Chico, Special Collection. (SC 13636)

Right: Willows' Giant Lemonade Stand. There was also one in Delevan. Courtesy Willows Museum.

WILLOWS RESOURCES

POINTS OF INTEREST
Willow Creek Wildlife Gallery- Country Road 48, (916) 934-5356
Willows Museum - 336 Walnut Street, (916) 934-8150
Willows Watering Hole Monument - Highway 165
Sacramento Northern Wildlife Refuge- Just south of Willows off old Highway 99
Delevan Wildlife Refuge - Between Maxwell and Willows
Blue Gum Inn- Highway 99W
Glenn County Court House
Willows Post Office- Registered as an historic building
Kanawha Four Corners - West of Willows on Elk Creek Road, site of Kanawha School
Willows Chamber of Commerce - 336 Walnut Street, (916) 934-8150
Willows Pheasant Association - (916) 934-3730
Glenn County Chamber of Commerce - (916) 934-7994

FESTIVALS and EVENTS
Lamb Derby Festival- Week before Mother's Day weekend
Willows Christmas Faire -Check with Chamber of Commerce

CAMPGROUNDS and RV PARKS
Stoney Gorge Reservoir - 28 miles west of Willows on Highway 162

ARTOIS

ARTOIS, once known as German-town, is between Willows and Orland, east of Interstate 5. It is said that during WW I a trainload of soldiers disembarked in this little hamlet, inhabited mostly by Germans, and literally tore the town apart, venting their war-time prejudices in a scene reminiscent of one in John Steinbeck's *East of Eden*. Shortly after the incident the town officially changed its name to Artois, named after a town in France, where many American soldiers were then fighting. The road leading to the tiny community offers an unusual sight: a warehouse painted bright pink. Remarkably, it is a beauty.

Germantown (Artois) in 1918. This photo was taken a little north of town, in an area called Rixville. Courtesy Willows Museum.

Union Hotel in Artois, before 1900. Courtesy Willows Museum.

ORLAND

ORLAND, WITH A population of 5,052 one of the larger towns in Glenn County, is a quiet farming community at the crossroads of Interstate 5, Highways 32 and 99W. Its fields are rich with olives, citrus, almonds, grains, fruits, vegetables and livestock.

During the 1940s Glenn County was the largest sheep producing county in the United States. Today Orland, with the neighboring town of Willows, celebrates the annual lamb festival in May, when celebrity chefs and thousands of visitors come to sample delicious barbecued lamb.

The first town site of the area, near Black Butte Dam, was called Newville, which grew to be an important trading center in the foothills. Its post office was established in 1868, but was closed in 1918. When the railroad came through the Sacramento Valley in the 1870s, most of Newville was simply relocated and renamed Orland. In 1976, Orland celebrated its centennial, just as the nation celebrated its 200th birthday.

Walker Street, Orland, circa 1890. Courtesy Meriam Library, California State University, Chico, Special Collection. (SC 6453)

The Orland Post Office and Drug Store, circa 1900. Courtesy Meriam Library, California State University, Chico, Special Collection. (SC 16421)

ORLAND RESOURCES

POINTS OF INTEREST
Black Butte Marina and Lake - Interstate 5 to Highway 32 west, (916) 865-2665
Southern Pacific Depot, Historic Train Engine, Tender and Caboose - Glenn
  County Fairgrounds in Orland
Heritage Trail - Glenn County Fairgrounds
Alta Schmidt House (museum) - 936 Fourth Street, (916) 865-5444

FESTIVALS AND EVENTS
Orland Craft Fair - Last weekend in November at Orland Memorial Hall
Glenn County Fair - County Fairgrounds, Orland

SHOPPING & FARM PRODUCTS
John Tolley - Road M, (916) 865-3155, citrus, cherries, nuts - November through February
Capay Satsuma Mandarin Orchard - Third and Cutting Ave.
Fariss Ranch - County Road P, December through March for navel oranges.
Shallow Creek Farm - (916) 865-4093, all year around, citrus and vegetables
Rudge's Roost - (916) 865-3629, May through October, vegetables, melons, and fruit
Nelson Ranch - (916) 865-9409, oranges
Martin's Navel Oranges - (916) 865-2151, citrus and tours
Rancho de Naranjas - (916) 865-2015, oranges
Ainsworth Orchards - (916) 865-3200, navel oranges
Bowen Orchards - (916) 865-4683 OR 865-5072, oranges, May through September

BED AND BREAKFAST INNS
The Inn at Shallow Creek Farms - County Road DD, Box 3179, (916) 865-4093

CAMPGROUNDS and RV PARKS
Hoff Ranch - RV overnight park, picnic area and oranges, (916) 865-3313
Koa Campground - County Road H, (916) 865-9188
Old Orchard RV Park - (916) 865-5335
Black Butte Lake - (916) 865-4781
Will Glenn Mobil - Highway 162 west, (916) 934-3193
Shady Oaks Trailer Court - County Road 99, (916) 865-0026
Orland Mobil and RV Park - County Road 99, (9160 865-2402

HAMILTON CITY

HAMILTON CITY, between Chico and Orland on Highway 32, is a settlement of 1, 811 people of several ethnic groups, who work the fruitful land as their forefathers did for almost 150 years. Nut and fruit orchards, grain fields and rows of sugar beets are the result of their labor.

Monroeville, about 4½ miles from Hamilton City on the east bank of the Sacramento River, once was the county seat of Colusi County (later changed to Colusa), which in 1850 encompassed present-day Colusa, Glenn, and part of Tehama Counties. In Monroeville, named for U.P. Monroe, the first building was built from the timbers and planks of a beached riverboat. In 1853, when the government offices transferred to Colusa, Monroeville reverted to being only a farm. Today students are trying to restore the historic old cemetery, which holds the grave of William Ide, the first and only president of the California Republic.

Jack Hauk, known as "Gasoline Jack," ran the first bus service between Chico and Hamilton City from 1911 to 1916. The first "bus" was a large open car that supposedly could carry up to 13 people, though exactly how this was done is not clear from this picture. When his business became more lucrative, Jack extended his route to Orland and later to Willows. Success afforded him the purchase of more bus-like vehicles, and he eventually changed his run from Chico to the mountain area of Westwood, often hauling workers to the lumber mills from the bus depot. Jack is the man standing outside the car; the driver was known as Red.
Courtesy John Nopel.

At the Sacramento Valley Sugar Company Picnic, July 4, 1906, some 2,000 people celebrated under the grove of trees southwest of the factory. Food, sports, various amusements, and factory tours were arranged for the event. "We believe that the number of strangers who visit us on occasion will largely increase the sale of lots in town and the general interest of the community and the opportunities for investments in the locality," proclaimed a spokesman for the sugar company, according to a note on the back of the photo. Courtesy Special Collection, Meriam Library, California State University, Chico. (SC 2005)

THE FLATLANDS

In the late 1930s, farming was often done with whatever equipment was available. Courtesy Jo Brubaker Cason.

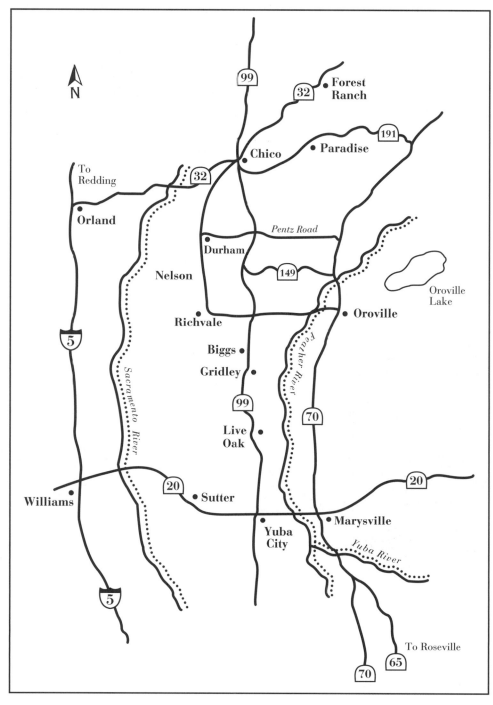

LIVE OAK

LIVE OAK, the northernmost town in Sutter County, is situated on the Feather River just 12 miles north of Yuba City. An early settler, George Baxter Meter, first called the area Antelope Ranch, for the thousands of antelope that roamed the area during the 1850s. The first house in Live Oak is said to have been built in 1869 by A.M. McGrew, who had purchased land from various squatters on the oak-studded flatland. In those days much of the surrounding land was wet and swampy during winter months, when the Feather River rose.

In 1865, the California and Oregon Railroad built a line through Live Oak, to connect Marysville to Portland, Oregon. Live Oak then became a thriving settlement. The first commercial building was built in 1874, a warehouse owned by C.E. Wilkinson. Today this quiet rural community has 4,320 residents.

W.H. Stafford's General Store, one of the first in Live Oak, Built by James Gilbert in 1878. The upper story was the Odd Fellows Hall. The building stands today, looking a little different. Courtesy Community Memorial Museum, Yuba City.

Live Oak around 1900. Fir Street looking east to the railroad tracks. Courtesy Memorial Museum, Yuba City.

IN THE 1850s such early farmers as George Bilhman and Hezekiah Luther came to the area and introduced quality crops like the French prune. For many years Live Oak has been considered one of the most fertile and best developed ranching areas in the valley. Cereal grains, beans, grapes, and almonds have been grown here for well over 100 years.

Inside the Live Oak meat market, circa 1910. On the left is owner W.R. Channon, father of local resident Mrs. James McElroy, and on the right is Clyde Hetrick. On the site today is a frozen food locker. Courtesy Marion McElroy.

Live Oak, circa 1910. The right half of building was a meat market owned by Sutter County Supervisor W.R. Channon, who stands in the center, wearing a white apron. The left side of the building is a restaurant, which later became a store, and then Dr. Higgins' office. Courtesy Marion McElroy.

THE LIVE OAK Church of the Brethren, built in 1912, stood next to the much older Live Oak Elementary School on Larkin Road. The church was later remodeled and additions were made for Sunday school rooms, still standing today. The first minister and cofounder of the church was the author's grandfather, W. R. Brubaker, who served as a rural mail carrier in the area for more than 30 years. A street was named in honor of him and his son, George.

Live Oak Church of the Brethren, circa 1912. A. Green Fillmore is standing in front.

The old white-washed grammar school building. Courtesy Evelyn Nesmith, granddaughter of W.R.. Brubaker.

George W. Landis family, 1890s. Back row from left: Minnie Landis (Hartman), Edith Landis (Reid), Cora. Front row: Rosetta Landis (Brubaker, married W.R. Brubaker), Ollie Landis, George W. Landis (a Dunkard preacher and farmer), Mary Landis (stepmother), and John Landis. Many descendants of this family reside in Live Oak and the surrounding counties. Author's collection.

72

Old Clay Grammar School, circa 1886, facing the west towards today's Highway 99 (put through in 1915). Note the stile for crossing the fence. The first school in Live Oak was built at the corner of Township Road and Pennington Road in 1865. The white-washed school-house was replaced in 1923 by a new brick school build-ing, which remains standing in part, and today houses a furniture store. Courtesy Marion McElroy.

Live Oak Elementary School pupils, about 1918. Teacher is Mrs. (Mary) Henry Stohlman. Fourth row (right end) is thought to be Rita Salisbury (Pasquini). Third row, second from right, is author's father, George W. Brubaker. Second row (last three people) are thought to be Virgil Terry, Velma Drew (Thayer) and Edith Wiser. All others unidentified. Courtesy Josephine M. Brubaker Cason.

Above: Live Oak boys in the National Guard. These Dough Boys served under General Pershing during the dispute between the United States and Mexico, and they later fought in World War I. All came home safely to their families. Left to right: Adams, Nelson, Gordon Clegg, later the town's grocer, and Ben Ricketts, who became the town barber. The other two are unidentified. Courtesy Marion McElroy.

Right: Jenny Hedger and her dog Sacto, circa 1910. Jenny was the first telephone operator in Live Oak. The telephone office was in the front part of her house, which stood next to the Odd Fellows Hall. W. H. Stafford was the first telephone manager, with some 26 customers by 1905. In 1909 F.A. Hedger took over the management. A road and school district were named after the Hedger family. Courtesy Marion McElroy.

IN THE CENTER of town along Highway 99, Live Oak proudly displays one of thirty-five Bi-centennial Live Oak Trees. These Valley Oaks have remained standing since our nation's constitution was signed. The northern Sacramento Valley was once densely shaded by this mighty oak tree, the *Quercus lobata*. Gradually the enormous trees were cut down and cleared away to open up the land for crops and to supply firewood for the river steamboats and for the railroad's steam engines.

Today the students of Live Oak Union High School honor the mighty oaks that once surrounded their home town, by calling their school annual, *The Quercus*.

First Home Economics class at Live Oak High School, held in the Live Oak Women's Club House, circa 1920.
Left to right: Edna Estelle, Marian Channon, Helen Tipton, unknown, Hope Salisbury, Florence Landis, unknown,
Rose Landis (behind), Eloise Ames, Thelma Wolf, Mabel Clark, Isabel Gratiot, teacher (standing).
Courtesy Marion McElroy.

LIVE OAK RESOURCES

POINTS OF INTEREST
Bi-Centennial Living Witness Trees- Over 200 years old and standing at the time the U.S. Constitution was signed. Located in Live Oak on Highway 99
Old Townsite of Pennington - West of Live Oak towards the Sutter Buttes.
Sutter Buttes - Take Pennington Road west

FESTIVALS
Live Oak Tree Festival - Third or fourth Saturday in September

SHOPPING & PRODUCE
Kiwi Ranch - Highway 99 (916) 695-1143, tours and kiwi products November through May
Mills Farm - 10580 O Street, (916) 695-2213, Kiwis, nuts, and prunes June through August
Key Berry Farm - 10646 Hedger Road, (916) 695-2297
Fruit Palace- At Lomo Crossing, 6205 Highway 99, (916) 695-1336
Al Perrin Ranch - 8272 Sheldon Road, (916) 695-2551, citrus, persimmons, nuts and grapes August through January

GRIDLEY

GRIDLEY, straddling Highway 99 about 15 miles north of Yuba City, is considered the Kiwi Capitol of the United States. Kiwi fruit was introduced some years ago from New Zealand, and now constitutes one of the major money crops in the area. This Butte County town of 4,631 boasts historic landmarks, friendly, well-maintained neighborhoods and a local Hispanic flavor. Gridley may be best known for the Gray Lodge Wildlife Refuge, one of the most active waterfowl marshlands in the United States.

In the 1850s, this area was considered to be an arid wasteland. George W. Gridley, the town's namesake, settled in the area and built up a prosperous sheep ranch. Using cheap Chinese labor, he cleared the land of the valley oak trees and brush, and planted grain. The actual town sprang up in the 1870s with the arrival of the railroad; it was incorporated in 1905.

Snowstorm at Gridley, January 27, 1916, corner of Hazel and Virginia Streets.
Courtesy Butte County Historical Society, Oroville, and Meriam Library, California State University, Chico, Special Collections. (SC10334).

The first fruit cannery in Butte County was established in May 1896, with Gridley's Hunts Cannery being the fore-runner of today's cannery. For years the cannery held its annual picnic, with dancing, carnival rides, circuses and barbecues. Today the Butte County Fair is held in Gridley. Above: Gridley cannery picnic, circa 1908. Courtesy Butte County Historical Society, Oroville, and Meriam Library, California State University, Chico, Special Collections. (SC 8992)

A RECIPE FOR HOW TO PRESERVE A HUSBAND
(with peaches and cream)

Be careful in your selection. Do not choose too young. When once select-ed, give your entire thought to preparation for domestic use. Some insist in keeping them in a pickle, others are constantly getting them into hot water. This may make them sour, hard and sometimes bitter. Even poor varieties may be made sweet, tender and good, garnishing them with patience, well sweetened with love and seasoned with kisses. Keep warm with a steady fire of domestic devotion and serve with peaches and cream. Thus prepared they will keep for years.

This old recipe is a reminder of county fairs. (author unknown)
Courtesy of the Native Daughters of the Golden West, Sutter Chapter.

GRIDLEY RESOURCES

POINTS OF INTEREST
Gray Lodge Wildlife Refuge- (916) 846-3315 -tours and special programs available
McCracken Bed and Breakfast - 1835 Sycamore Street, (916) 846-2108
Thresher Mansion - Bed and Breakfast Inn, (916) 846-0630
Silk Stocking Row - Hazel Street with all its historic homes
Chamber of Commerce - (916) 846-3146

FESTIVALS
Red Suspender Days - Third weekend, Friday through Sunday in May
California Rice Festival in Gridley - At the fairgrounds in June, check with Chamber of Commerce
Gridley's Historic Home Tour - October, (916) 846-3146
Festival of Trees - November, (916) 846-3146
Coot Scoot - Gray Lodge Wildlife Refuge in April, (916) 846-3316

SHOPPING & FARM PRODUCTS
Johnson's Backyard Produce - 446 Hopkins Avenue, October - April, kiwi, tomatoes and walnuts
Stowe Ranch - 882 East Evans Reimer Road, (916) 846-5538 - mail order kiwis and peaches
Boeger Ranch - (916) 846-2104 or 846-2044, pears
Wi-Ker-Ser Kiwi Fruit Ranch - 661 East Evans Reimer Road, (916) 846-6664
Kiwi Blossom Packing- 192 Highway 99, (916) 695-1448
Monney Farms - (916) 846-0906, showroom, mail order, gift packs, kiwi products, fruits and berries
J & R Produce - Highway 70, popcorn, apples, avocados, strawberries
Irwin Apple Ranch - 370 O'Brien, (916) 846-4414

Simpson and Sons Wagon and Blacksmith Shop and Chapman and Williams Carriage Painters, on the corner of Washington and Hazel Streets, circa 1890. Today the building houses Gridley Plumbing. Courtesy Butte County Historical Society, Oroville and Meriam Library, California State University, Chico, Special Collections.

BIGGS

BIGGS, A QUIET and pretty hamlet of 1,581 people located a few miles northwest of Gridley, grew up in the 1870s as a grain shipping center on the railroad route connecting major cities to the north and south. Biggs at one time had the only train depot between Live Oak and Chico. Farmers like Col. Frances M. Biggs, the town's namesake, and George Gridley relied on the railroad to transport their sheep, wool, lumber and grain. Biggs in the late 1890s was the site of a fruit cannery shipping canned fruit by rail.

The town's main street has examples of architecture from decades past, from Victorian-style houses to bungalows to the 1950s stucco and modern ranch style homes. The tiny downtown business district has an ambience of the 1930s that blends very well with the residential area.

View of Main Street in Biggs from the waterworks tower, circa 1890.
Courtesy California Section, California State Library in Sacramento.

RICHVALE

As its name implies, Richvale, off Highway 99 between Gridley and Chico, is a valley rich with the golden grains of California. Grain silos dot the otherwise flat horizon. The Lundberg family, makers of well-known rice products, are leaders in the rice-growing industry. Like many families of this region, they came to this fertile land during the dust bowl days to put their farming skills to use.

The Sacramento Valley has the ideal climate and terrain to produce high quality rice. Eight counties in the valley bring up to $600 million annually into the economy through rice production. Supplying the United States with 20% of its rice, the crop also produces enough oxygen for one half of California's 30 million people.

Rice was first commercially grown in the Sacramento Valley in 1912, when the land was leveled by horse and plow and seeding was done by a grain drill or "Broad-caster Seeder" that spread the seed over the ground. Some farmers flooded their fields before seeding while other watered afterwards. At harvest time, rice binders were brought in and the rice was cut and stacked into 5 to 6 bundles to allow uniform drying. Stationary rigs, run by pulley belts connected to a tractor, were then hauled to the fields to thresh the crop, which was then sacked. Later the swather and mobile harvester or combine were used for reaping the crops.

Steam threshers, near Richvale (Selsby Switch), circa 1900. These appear to be combines, which cut and thresh the grain in a single operation. Steam threshers had large boiler tanks that were fueled with wood, throwing up fine clouds of smoke and steam. Courtesy Special Collection, Meriam Library, California State University, Chico. (SC 5908)

RICHVALE RESOURCE
Lundberg Family Farms - Richvale, Ca 95974-0369

Crop dusting and flagman, circa 1937.
Courtesy California State Library, Sacramento, Curry collection. (Neg. # 3488)

NELSON

NELSON SITS BETWEEN Richvale and Durham among flowing rice fields. The remote settlement has only a combination store and post office station, a few weathered houses and out-buildings. As the rice industry began to flourish in the early 1900s, farmers from the various parts of the country came to the valley in search of open, flat fields with rich soil. Ground that had been prepared for grain in the mid 1800s proved ideal for raising rice. Nelson was one such place.

Rice farming was revolutionized with new seeding and fertilizing techniques. "High-tech" machinery and scientifically advanced equipment are now used to prepare and plant the land. Lasers and computers now show how to level the land precisely, so that critically uniform depths of water can be maintained without endangering California's precious water supply.

Prepared fields are flooded with 2 to 4 inches of water from rivers or reservoirs, awaiting the fly-over seeding by crop planes. The crop dusting plane is used throughout the season to apply fertilizers and crop protectants. Once the water is drained and the land is dry, combines arrive to harvest the rice, which is then shipped to warehouses for slow drying. Rice stubble from harvested fields is then burned to prevent fungi from being passed to next year's crop.

Today it is a common sight to see crop dusting planes fly over the flatlands discharging their payloads. California rice growers are more technically advanced than those of any other country.

DURHAM

DURHAM LIES OFF the beaten path on the Dayton-Durham Highway, about 15 miles south of Chico in Butte County, among the green pastures of cattle country and the open fields of grain.

In 1844, Samuel Neal and David Dutton acquired a grant from the Mexican government on Butte Creek, near present-day Durham. Robert W. Durham, Neal's companion, received 240 acres of the Esquon Grant when Samuel Neal died. The magnificent remains of the old Robert Durham homestead still stand today on the Dayton-Durham Highway a little way past the railroad tracks.

This area was first known as Butte Valley in 1861, but upon construction of the railroad, the town of Durham was established in 1871. Robert Durham, the second postmaster, was the founder. Today the town, with 4,784 residents, is experiencing some welcome growth.

Snow in Durham in 1937. Courtesy Meriam Library, Special Collection, California State University, Chico. (SC 6732)

Durham's "Colony School Bus", circa 1920. A note on the photograph says this bus served the Durham land colony children. In the winter-time a canvas roof was put up. Agnes Pearce is one of the young ladies on the bus. Courtesy Meriam Library, California State University, Chico, Special Collections. (SC 6753)

Ranch hands tending cattle, near Durham, 1930.
Courtesy Meriam Library, California State University, Chico, Special Collections. (SC 6707)

DURHAM RESOURCES

Books Pumpkin Patch - 8975 Highway 99 about 1 mile south of
  Durham exit or Pentz Road, (916) 893-8783. Open for month of October
  with tours, picnic area, horse drawn rides, pumpkins, honey, popcorn and
  more.
Durham Harvest Festival - September, (916) 343-8969
Almond Blossom Run - February, (916) 345-1000
Blacksmith Shop -(100 years old)
Old Durham Homestead and Sam Neal's Rancho Esquon - Out of Durham
  on the Dayton-Durham Highway, left past the railroad tracks
La Flesh Enterprises - 9731 Lott Road, (916) 343-1848, English walnuts

Yes, California still has cowboys
and ranch hands. The flatland area
has been used to raise fine herds of
cattle, horses, sheep, goats and even
some buffalo at one time. Butte
County's Table Mountain Ranch,
for example, offers fine grazing
during the spring and summer
months.

CHICO

CHICO, 100 miles north of Sacramento, is a university town that is growing at a rate of three times the national average, with a population today of 40,079. The diversified community is blessed with prosperous businesses, a California State University, light industry, various types of farming and plenty of outdoor recreation. Yet, with all these features, Chico still has that small-town, friendly, personal atmosphere.

Early settlers traveling north up the fertile Sacramento Valley were attracted by two babbling creeks, the Big and Little Chico Creeks. Chico grew up between them, and

has flourished as a healthy city with an expansive park system. Many of the town's historic buildings have been preserved as a reminder of the settlement's early and proud beginnings.

John Bidwell, one of California's earliest pioneers, was a member of the first party of immigrants to cross the Sierras to California in 1841. Bidwell, manager of John Sutter's Hock farm, made a rich gold strike on the Feather River near Oroville (Bidwell Bar), with which he purchased Rancho del Arroyo Chico in 1860. In the early days, Rancho Chico was known for its wine-producing grapes, on vines which were later destroyed. It was said that Bidwell cultivated up to four hundred different fruit trees.

He donated much of his land for schools, parks, and churches. Bidwell was a member of the first California Senate in 1849 and was elected to Congress in 1865.

Bidwell and his wife, Annie Kennedy Bidwell, built a splendid Italianate house in Chico, the equal of any dwelling of the time in San Francisco or Sacramento, featuring a four-story square tower and an encircling veranda. Today a state historical museum, the house recalls the words of a plaintive American folk song about the westering movement, *Down in the Valley* : "Build me a castle/ Forty feet high/ So I can see you/ As you ride by." One can imagine Annie Bidwell in her magnificent house, watching her husband ride by.

Probably the earliest photograph in this book shows the Chico Store and Post Office, located on Rancho Chico, circa 1852. Courtesy Meriam Library, California State University, Chico, Special Collections. (SC 11181)

Bidwell's Mansion before the landscaping, circa 1870. This beautiful Italianate Victorian house is now a museum, one of California's most important historic buildings. Courtesy Butte County Historical Society and Meriam Library, California State University, Chico, Special Collection. (SC 4082)

John and Annie Kennedy Bidwell.
Courtesy California Room, Yuba County Library, Marysville.

WHEN John Bidwell traveled north from Bidwell Bar to purchase Rancho del Arroyo Chico (later shortened to Rancho Chico, "The Ranch by the Little Stream") in 1849, he had visions of making the parcel a prosperous estate. To prepare the fertile land for farming, he used the local Indians residing on the rancheria. These natives were of the Mechoopdas tribe (Chico Maidus), who lived in low, dome-shaped structures. Caves dug in the ground were covered with a thatched roof covered with mud and a small hole at the top for a chimney.

Bidwell's humane treatment of the Indians was somewhat unusual for the times. He provided clothing and shoes to his workers as a concerned gesture for their protection and safety as well as modesty. (These articles were not necessarily seen as comfortable by the Indians). When John married Annie Kennedy and brought her to the ranch, she took an immediate interest in the Indians' education, religion, and the development of their skills. Mrs. Bidwell established an industrial school where Indians learned to cut, sew and make their own clothing.

In 1863 many of the Chico Ranch Indians, along with other Maidus, were sent by the government to the Round Valley Reservation. Annie Bidwell, who always had an open door policy for the ranch Indians, wanted to make provisions for them upon her death. She deeded two parcels of land to the Presbyterian Church for management on behalf of the Indians, but the land reverted back to the estate in 1921. Eventually 14 acres of the rancheria were awarded to Chico State University, and $80,000 paid to the Mechoopda tribe. After many legal transactions, only a tiny cemetery belongs to the Mechoopda tribe, and only one small parcel of land is still owned by a Chico Maidu descendant.

Below: Mrs. Susan Clement, a 100-year-old woman who lived on the Chico Rancheria. Courtesy Bidwell Mansion State Park and Meriam Library, California State University, Chico, Special Collections. (SC 6346)

Above: Chico Rancheria Indian family, circa 1910. A note on the photograph says that the family name is Conway, Jody and Isaiah standing with Dewey in the mother's lap. Courtesy Bidwell Mansion State Park & Meriam Library, California State University, Chico, Special Collections. (SC 11726)

Chico State College, now a state university, circa 1940. Founded in 1889, it is the second oldest institution in the state university system. Courtesy California Room, Yuba County Library, Marysville.

Chico State Normal School, the forerunner to the present university, circa 1897. The purpose of a Normal School was to train teachers. The land for the Normal School was donated by John Bidwell; the Bidwell Mansion was once used as a campus dormitory. Courtesy Bidwell Mansion State Historic Park and Meriam Library, California State University, Chico, Special Collections. (SC 11728)

Chico Soda Works at 5th and Ivy Streets, 1910. Owner A.G. Eames owned the wholesale business that sold those old favorite soda drinks like root beer, sarsaparilla, orange soda and Delaware punch, along with 50-pound blocks of ice. The company, originally called Blood's Crystal Soda Works, was started by A.F. Blood in 1870 on 7th and Broadway, but relocated in 1895 when purchased by Eames, who lived in the house shown to the right. The heavy blocks of ice would be delivered to residents' homes and placed in the ice box by icemen using tongs. By 1930 and 1940, when electric refrigerators replaced ice boxes and large bottling companies out-produced the small wholesalers, icemen and Delaware punch passed into history. Coca Cola or Nehi Orange became the things to drink, and small ice cubes could be frozen in the electric refrigerator. Courtesy John Nopel and Meriam Library, California State University, Chico, Special Collection. (SC 2795)

Opposite, below: The famed 200-year-old Sir Joseph Hooker Oak Tree shrouded in snow, with Mr. and Mrs. Jules E. Gerbardt, 1920s. Named for a famous botanist who visited Chico, the Hooker Oak, "the largest tree of its kind in the world," stood tall and mighty, measuring 110 feet high with a spread of 150 feet. When the tree fell in 1977, it was found to have been actually two trees grown together. Courtesy Butte County Historical Society, Oroville and Meriam Library, California State University, Chico, Special Collections. (SC 4079)

Above: Main Street Chico, 1920s. Chico for years has been the region's major trade center.
Courtesy California Room, Yuba County Library, Marysville.

CHICO RESOURCES

POINTS OF INTEREST
Bidwell Park - 2250 acres - picnicking, swimming, horseback riding, golf, jogging trails and more.
  The fourth largest municipal park in the United States.
Bidwell Mansion Historic Park- 525 Esplanade, (916) 895-6144, tours
California State University, Chico - Normal Street
Sierra Nevada Brewing Company - 2539 Cilman Way, (915) 893-3520, tours
Stansbury Home - 307 W. 5th Street, (916) 895-3848, tours
Museum of Anthropology - California State University, Chico, September - May, (916) 895-5397
Chico Creek Nature Center and Deer Pens - Bidwell Park ,Tuesday - Saturday
Centerville Museum - Humbug Road in the historic town of Centerville, between Chico and Paradise
Chico Museum - 2nd and Salem Streets
Honey Run Covered Bridge - Built in 1894, Humbug Road in Butte Creek Canyon
Greater Chico Chamber of Commerce - 500 Main Street, (916) 891-5556
Chico Area Recreation & Park District (Card) - (916) 895-4711
Historic Pedicab Tours -(916) 343-3130
Gem and Mineral Museum - 950 Muir, (916) 343-3839

FESTIVALS
Robin Hood Days - August Celebration of 1930s film making, (916) 891-5556
Multi - Cultural Day - In May, (916) 343-5210
Latin American Music Festival - Second Saturday in May, 300 Wall Street
Fiesta de la Mansion and Almond Festival - Bidwell Mansion Park - September, (916) 895-6144
Chico Air Show and Antique Fly - In - September, (916) 891-5556

SHOPPING & FARM PRODUCTS
Orient and Flume Glass Blowers- 2161 Park Avenue, (916) 893-0373 magnificent hand-blown glass objects
Blue Diamond Growers - 703 Miller Avenue, (916) 895-1853, nuts and gift packs
Chico Farmer's Market - E. 6th and Orient Streets, (916) 345-8569
T.J. Farms - 3600 Chico Avenue, (916) 343-2294, nuts, kiwi, jams and vinegars. Gift packs and mail orders
Weiss Kiwi Fruit - 594 Paseo Road, Campaneros, November - December
Wahl Ranch - 3195 Dayton-Durham Highway, nuts and flavored almonds
Abbey Acres - (916) 345-1048, vegetables, herbs, nuts
Callender Farm - (916) 342-4355, mail order, gift packs, nuts, fruit, rice, jellies, vinegars
Tropicana West - (916) 893-4514, specialty fruits and gift packs
Day To Day Orchards- (916) 342-2547, nuts and feijoas
Bond's Garden Produce - (916) 1479 or 893-1226, June - December, pumpkins, vegetables and gourmet popcorn

BED AND BREAKFAST INNS
Bullard House -256 East First Avenue, (916) 342-5912
Music Express Bed & Breakfast - 1091 El Monte Avenue, (916) 891-9833
Camelot - (916) 343-9164
O'Flaherty House Bed & Breakfast - (916) 893-5494
The Palms - 1525 Dayton Road
Johnson's Country Inn - 3935 Morehead Avenue, (916) 345-7829

CAMPING FACILITIES
Butte Meadows - Highway 32 east to the Butte Meadows

THE RIDGE

M. J. Coney, Diamond Mine promoter at Oroville. In 1853 the first U. S. diamond discovery was made outside of Oroville in the little mining town of Cherokee, settled by an Oklahoma school teacher and his Cherokee Indian students. The mine, which yielded only low-grade diamonds, never proved profitable. Mr. Coney also operated the Goldbank Mine in Forbestown in 1912. Courtesy Yuba Feather Historical Association, Forbestown.

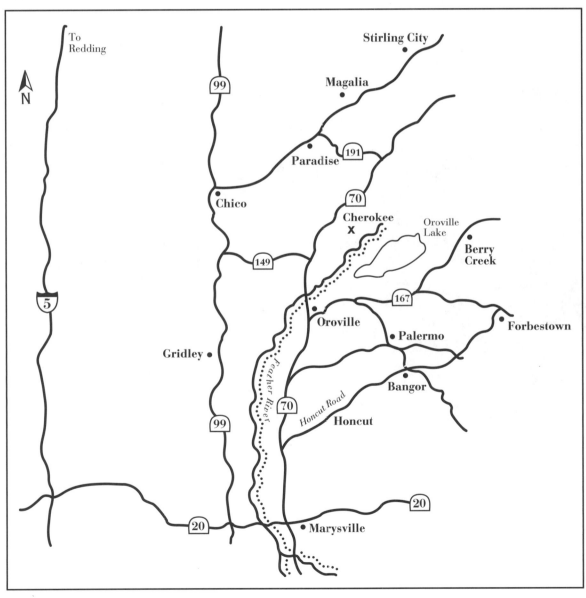

OROVILLE

OROVILLE, whose name is inseparable from gold rush history, was once called the "Wickedest Town in California". The thriving mining town drew people from all walks of life and all parts of the country. With more than 4,000 inhabitants, it had more saloons per capita than any other town in the state. In those days prices were high; 100 pounds of flour cost $60, 50 pounds of sugar, $75, and a keg of whiskey $4,500. Ophir City, the town's first name which came from the legendary Arabian land of gold, also had a Chinese population of some 10,000 (usually not included in the town population figures). The Chinese Joss house in Oroville, built in 1863, is said to be the oldest such Chinese temple in America.

The tent town of Oroville grew fast after the discovery of gold by John Bidwell at Bidwell Bar, which has been under water since the Oroville Dam was built. Today the oldest suspension bridge in the world spans the Feather River gorge. Across the road from the old toll house, at the end of the bridge, the "Mother Orange Tree," planted in 1856, is said to have started the citrus fruit industry in Northern California. In that same year, Oroville was considered to be the fifth largest city in the state and the largest mining camp in the west.

Oroville, the county seat of Butte County, sits near the junction of the North, Middle and South forks of the Feather River. To protect the areas below from flooding, the massive Oroville dam, the largest earth-filled dam in the world, was built in 1968. Oroville lake, behind the dam, has become an attractive recreation area for the fisher, skier, boater, camper, and 33,531 residents.

A 20-horse team in front of the Great American Importing Tea Company, downtown Oroville, circa 1890.
Courtesy Butte County Historical Society, Oroville, and Meriam Library,
California State University, Chico, Special Collections. (SC 9422)

Gold digging dredger.
Courtesy California Room, Yuba County Library, Marysville.

THE FIRST SUCCESSFUL gold dredger was built in 1898 by Resdon Iron Works of San Francisco for operation on the Feather River near Oroville. W.P. Hammon, who had an interest in Yuba Consolidated Goldfields at Hammonton, near Marysville, also brought in his equipment. The river near Oroville has floated more dredgers than any other place in California. At one time 45 of the monster machines worked within sight of each other. In the early 1900s the only known would-be gold robbery on a dredger failed when the robber held the crew at gun point, but lost his nerve and ran off.

Almost one hundred years later, the piles of rock and gravel along Highway 70 are a shameful reminder of the defacing of the land when dredgers were used to dig the bottom of the Feather River in search of gold. Fortunately some creative uses have been found for the piles of gravel. Oroville rid itself of some 150 million tons of the rubble to construct the Oroville Dam, and Marysville, in building its levee system, used many thousands of tons of rocks and boulders.

When thousands of gold seekers had flocked to the area in 1848 and Oroville became a tent-city overnight. Within a few years cattle ranches began to dot the land lying at the base of the Sierra Nevada Mountain Range. Some of the unlucky and discouraged miners to search elsewhere for their fortunes, while many more stayed on to develop the land and the community. Trees were harvested and the lumber industry brought new prosperity. Sawmills were built, offering work to local townsmen, and the olive packing industry was born in the early years of the new century.

In 1910, the Postmaster General installed a postal savings system in communities with large payrolls, enabling workers to deposit their money in a savings account at the nearby post office. With large payrolls from both the dredging and the lumbering businesses, Oroville was selected as the first city in the state to have a postal savings facility.

The Oroville Post Office in the I.O.O.F. building on Montgomery Street, circa 1911. Will Leonard, Postmaster, is standing behind the woman in the white dress. Note the woman wearing sleeve protectors. Courtesy Oroville Post Office.

I.O.M.,(?) circa 1892. Front row left to right: Jessie Leonard, President, later married to John Godfrey; Lillie Smith, Secretary; and Millie Tucker, who died of consumption in 1894; and members Ella Wilcox, Helen Houser, Fannie Wyld, and Ida Reagan. Courtesy Meriam Library, California State University, Chico, Special Collection. (SC10354)

THE EHMANN FAMILY, who had a very successful ripe-olive packing industry in Oroville, sold their products all over the world. Frieda Ehmann perfected her curing formula, which brought competitive olive processing plants to Oroville. Today the Ehmann Olive Packaging Plant is located on Lincoln Street.

Mrs. Ehmann and her son built a house on the corner of Lincoln and Robinson streets. After the family relocated in the bay area, the County bought the house to be used for county offices. In 1980 the Butte County Historical Society acquired the Ehmann House as a gift from the County. It is now on the National Register of Historic Buildings, and is used not only as a museum of Butte County's historic artifacts, but also as a library.

Frieda Ehmann examining her olives, circa 1915. Courtesy Butte County Historical Society, Oroville, and Special Collections, Meriam Library, California State University, Chico. (SC 9934).

The Ehmann house, today is the home of the Butte County Historical Society, housing artifacts, a library and olive gift packs. Sandy Shepherd, photographer.

AN IMPORTANT historic figure of Oroville is Ishi, the last Yahi Indian. In 1911, at the age of about 50, Ishi wandered into Oroville from his people's land in the surrounding mountains, into a modern world of which he knew very little. He became a ward of the famous professor of anthropology, Alfred Kroeber, at the University of California in Berkeley, where he lived for some years after his "discovery." Several books have been written about the mystery of his existence, his language, and his membership in a tribe thought to have been extinct for many years. Today in Oroville an historic monument honors this brave Yahi Indian.

Ishi posed for this picture on the day of his discovery at the Oroville Slaughterhouse on August 29, 1911. The photograph was taken by Adolph Kessler. Courtesy of the Meriam Library, California State University, Chico, Special Collection. (SC 3643)z

Below: The first automobile to visit Oroville in 1890. Courtesy Meriam Library, California State University, Chico, Special Collections. (SC 16895)

OROVILLE RESOURCES

POINTS OF INTEREST
C.F. Lott Home - 1067 Montgomery Street, (916) 533-2497 at Sank Park - Victorian house and tours
Oroville Chinese Temple - Built in 1863, 1500 Broderick Street, (916) 533-1496 -tours
Cherokee Museum - Gold mining artifacts from world's largest hydraulic mining site (916) 533-1849
Butte County Pioneer Memorial Museum - 2332 Montgomery Street, (916) 532-0107
Bidwell Bar Toll House Museum - Lake Oroville State Recreation Area (916) 538-2200
Oregon City Museum - In historic Oregon City off Highway 70, next to old school across covered bridge
Feather River Fish Hatchery - (916) 538-2222
The Ehmann House - Robinson and Lincoln Streets, museum and library
The Oroville Dam - Tours available
The Suspension Bridge- Oroville Lake Recreation Area, (916) 538-2219
The "Mother Orange Tree" - At the suspension bridge
Feather River Falls Scenic Area - Plunging 640 feet over a cliff, the sixth highest fall in the United States
Butte Junior College - Durham - Pentz Road
The Last Yahi Landmark - Corner Oro-Quincy Highway and Oak Street

FESTIVALS
Bidwell Bar Day - First Saturday in May
Frontier Christmas - First Saturday in December, (916) 538-2219
Admission Day Celebration - (916) 538-2200
Oroville Feather Fiesta Days - (916) 533-2542
Oroville Blues and Cultural Festival - First weekend in July, (916) 534-1081
Wild Mountain Faire - In Concow, the month of June, music, crafts, games, (916) 534-7792 or 534-5947
California State Old - Time Fiddler's Association Contest- March, (916) 533-2111
Rattlesnake Days and Craft Fair - Butte Community College - (916) 895-2509

SHOPPING & FARM PRODUCTS
Oroville Farmer's Market - Meyers Street, on Thursdays, May through November, (916) 534-6216
Oak Ranch - 97 Oakdale Avenue, (916) 534-9104, organically grown oranges
Fry's Pecans - 965 Lindsey Lane, (916) 534-0406
Kelso's Black Gold Ranch - 1161 Mt. Ida Road, (916) 589-1648, almonds, mandarins
Yankee Hill Farms - (916) 534-3343, kiwi, wreaths, herbs, and dried flowers
Hicks' Navel Oranges - (916) 589-0577, December - February
Brennan Berry Farm - (916) 533-7081, berries, vegetables, and plants, mail order.

BED AND BREAKFAST INNS
Jean Pratt's Riverside Bed & Breakfast - 1124 Middlehoff Lane, (916) 533-1413
River Haven Hideaway Bed & Breakfast - 1112 Middlehoff Lane, (916) 534-3344
Montgomery Bed & Breakfast Inn - 1400 Montgomery Street, (916) 532-1400
Lake Oroville Bed & Breakfast - 240 Sunday Drive, (916) 589-0700

CAMPGROUNDS & RV PARKS
Oroville Lake State Recreation Area - (916) 534-2049
Caribou Campground - (916) 283-0956
B & J Campground - (916) 533-1995

Palermo school, circa 1890. Courtesy Meriam Library,
California State University, Chico, Special Collections.(SC 16797)

PALERMO

Palermo is a town of 5,260 people, situated about five miles south of Oroville off Highway 70, and lying at the foot of the Sierras. Palermo and Oroville were part of the Northern Citrus Belt in the 1890s. The climate and soil were much like those along the Mediterranean, making the area perfect for growing oranges and lemons, as well as figs, prunes, peaches, pears, quince, grapes and olives.

In the 1860s realtors from San Francisco, planning to create a kind of agricultural paradise, subdivided 7,000 acres in Palermo and called it the Palermo Citrus Colony. One of the first investors and growers was Senator George Hearst, father of William Randolph Hearst, who was joined by other prominent and wealthy men.

Palermo, already a thriving farming settlement, grew faster when the railroad came through the fertile land in the 1870s. Once the depot was built, the local orchardists could ship their crops to distant markets. Still standing is the historic house used as the headquarters of the Palermo Citrus Colony, today a private home.

PALERMO RESOURCE
Palermo Field Days - September, (916) 534-6565, pancake breakfast, parade, auction, games and music

---

BANGOR

BANGOR is nestled snugly in the rolling foothills southwest of Oroville. Once a thriving mining camp, Bangor today is a quiet little roadside community dotted with oak trees, consisting of a school, a lovely church dating from 1882, a post office, store, gas station and bar.

Bangor was settled in 1855 by J.R. and Samuel Lumbert, who opened up a store for miners. The town grew slowly until a mine struck blue lead. Soon tents and shanties dotted the land. Then came three hotels, several stores, a bank, a school and dozens of saloons. During the peak of the gold rush days, when thousands of Chinese lived in Marysville and Oroville, Bangor too had a sprinkling of them. Resentment toward Chinese immigrants was strong in those early years, and it was claimed that the Chinese were robbed daily in Oroville and the Bangor area. But in 1857 when several men murdered a Chinese man from Bangor, the miners banded together to bring justice to the victim by hanging the guilty parties. The old hanging tree stood until the 1970s, when it was chopped down. As time passed and mines gave out, the population of Bangor dwindled down to about 400 people. Only an abandoned mine shaft remains today, whispering the tale of the town's early history.

Main Street in Bangor with the Miner's Saloon, Harness Shop and Shoe Shop, circa 1875. Standing in front of the buildings are John Nelson and Jim Hedge. Courtesy Community Memorial Museum, Yuba City.

Bangor School children, circa 1890. Note the variety of clothing, and two teachers, one for boys, one for girls. Courtesy Meriam Library, California State University, Chico, Special Collection. (SC 8927)

BERRY CREEK

BERRY CREEK, in eastern Butte County, is blessed with scenic canyons and magnificent waterfalls. This beautiful pine-studded mountain community of about 2,000 souls was also the site of some dredging operations in earlier days. It is hard to imagine that man's lust for gold could disturb this wondrous countryside. Rock-hounds and gem hunters who trek toward Feather Falls on Lumpkin Road may find plentiful quartz crystals and chlorite inclusions.

Near Berry Creek are two great natural wonders. Off the Forbestown Road a path leads to Feather Falls, at 640 feet the sixth highest waterfall on the United States mainland. It is second in California only to Yosemite Falls. Seven miles of marked hiking trails lead the vis-itor to the falls and back in approximately four hours. The last mile to the waterfalls is steep, requiring proper shoes and clothing, drinking water and hiking knowledge.

Bald Rock, a unique formation where native Americans left their grinding marks, is reached by the Bald Rock Road, past Berry Creek. It affords a magnificent view of the Sacramento Valley and coastal mountains.

First hotel at Berry Creek, circa 1890.
Courtesy Butte County Historical Society, Oroville, and Meriam Library, California State University, Chico, Special Collections. (SC 10355)

Challenge Mill near Merrimac. Merrimac, once a bustling lumber camp where enormous pine and fir trees were harvested, today is only a sparsely populated mountainside spot on the road to Berry Creek, distinguished only by its past. Courtesy Plumas County Museum, Quincy.

BERRY CREEK RESOURCES

Lake Oroville Bed & Breakfast Inn - 240 Sunday Drive, (916) 589-0700
Mountain House - 9 miles north of Berry Creek (thought to be Black Bart's hideout)
Feather Falls - North of Berry Creek off of Forbestown Road
Bald Rock - Highway 162 north of Berry Creek
Little North Fork Campground - (916) 534-6500
Milsap Bar Campground - (916) 534-6500
Rogers Cow Camp - (916) 534-6500
Oroville Aviation - Provide flying tours over Feather Falls

PARADISE

PARADISE SITS well above the fog, in the midst of splendid scenery that presumably earned the town its name. But one story claims that the town was named in the mining era for the Pair-O-Dice Saloon. Paradise, with a population of 25,408, is the largest of the communities that ride the "Ridge". Butte Creek has actually cut the Sierra Nevada Mountain Range in two at the Butte Creek Canyon area, leaving perpendicular rock walls hundreds of feet high and giving the rugged rock formation the distinctive name known as the "Ridge". The pine-scented retirement community is rich in cultural events, with a popular local theater company and shops full of arts, crafts and antiques.

Sometimes called "The Little Grand Canyon" by the locals, Butte Creek Canyon lies midway between Paradise and Chico. A narrow winding road leads to the historic mining towns of Diamondville and Centerville. The Centerville schoolhouse, built in 1894, still stands and was in operation until 1966. Nearby is one of the first hydro-electric power plants erected in California, still in use by Pacific Gas and Electric Company.

The Paradise and Magalia (Dogtown) area grew rapidly after Chauncy Wright found California's largest gold nugget in 1859. It was nearly a foot long, similar in shape to Africa, and sold in San Francisco for a sum of $10,690. The claim where the nugget was discovered brought in another $30,000 worth of gold in just ten days. Along with mining, the lumbering industry also flourished for years on the Ridge.

In 1901 the Diamond Match Company purchased 70,000 acres of timberland in order to expand their match industry. Barber, one mile south of Chico, was the site chosen for the factory, and a town to be named Stirling City was to be the site of the new sawmill. The ravine near today's Stirling City was convenient for a log pond. The company built the Butte County Railroad in 1904 to connect the mountain sawmill to the flatland manufacturing plant. This railroad line became the Stirling City Branch of Southern Pacific in 1915. Although the railroad was built mainly to haul timber, it also carried passengers. For mountain residents, the one-hour trip to Barber was a blessed relief from the previous transportation methods, which required an overnight stay in Chico.

Olive Street in Paradise, July 4, 1916. Courtesy Butte County Historical Society, Oroville, and Meriam Library, California State University, Chico, Special Collections. (SC 11372)

THE STIRLING CITY depot burned down in 1939; the Magalia and Paradise depots were used until 1960 and remain standing today. The closure of the Butte County Railroad began with Stirling City, when the sawmill closed in 1958. But the tracks and sawmill were reopened for ten more years between 1964-1974 when the Diamond Match Company opened a stud mill in Stirling City. The tracks were finally removed in 1979, and the grades near Paradise and on top of the ridge are now hiking and riding trails.

Butte County Railroad, Engine No. 3 in the snow at the Magalia Depot. No. 3, a second-hand engine purchased by BCRR, was a small 4-4-0 type American Standard locomotive, built in 1887. It was intended for the lighter loads such as passengers rather than massive lumber cargoes. Courtesy John Nopel and Meriam Library, California State University, Chico, Special Collection.

Paradise school, circa 1910. The school was built prior to 1889 at the corner of Elliott and Copeland Roads. Teachers were Ben Helphenstine, teaching the upper four grades, and Lola Van Ness, instructing the first four grades; she looks exhausted, perhaps from the effort of arranging all the children by height. Ira Charlton began teaching at this school in January 1911, with an enrollment of 48 pupils. Courtesy Meriam Library, California State University, Chico, Special Collections. (SC 11831)

The Paradise Hotel (right), now an antique shop, and Gulielsa Store (left), on Black Olive Street, 1920. Courtesy Butte County Historical Society, Oroville, and Meriam Library, California State University, Chico, Special Collection. (SC 11377)

PARADISE RESOURCES

POINTS OF INTEREST
Gold Nugget Museum - 502 Pearson Road, (916) 872-8722
Centerville Museum - 13544 Centerville Road in Butte Creek Canyon, (916) 342-9124
Paradise Art Center - 5564 Almond Street, (916) 877-9830
Hot Air Balloon Rides - Sierra Nevada Ballooning Co. (916) 872-4509
Chamber of Commerce (Paradise and Allied Communities) - (916) 877-9356

FESTIVALS AND EVENTS
Gold Nugget Days - Third or Fourth weekend in April (Thursday - Sunday)
Johnny Appleseed Days - First Saturday in October, (916) 877-9356
Paradise Performing Arts Festival - May or June. Check with Chamber of Commerce
Antique Show and Sale - March. Check with Chamber of Commerce
Great Northern Dixieland Jazz Festival - First weekend in June, (916) 877-1733
Gem and Mineral Show - April, (916) 872-1983

SHOPPING & PRODUCE
Gerten's Gardens - (916) 877-6436, apples and apple head dolls.
Noble Orchard Co. - 7050 Pentz Road, (916) 877-4784, apples

BED AND BREAKFAST INNS & LODGES
Inskip Inn - P.O. Box 68, Stirling City, Ca. (916) 873-0804
Sterling City Hotel - 16975 Skyway, Stirling City, Ca. (916) 873-0858
Canyon Shadows Bed & Breakfast - 12459 Centerville Road, Centerville, Ca. (916) 345-5461

CAMPGROUNDS AND RV PARKS
Pine Ridge Park - (916) 877-9677
Feather West Travel Park (916) 877-9666
Quail Trails Village - (916) 877-6581

MAGALIA

MAGALIA, the little settlement up on the ridge above Paradise, once had the unattractive name of "Dog Town." In early days the little hamlet was officially called Butte Mills, but became better known by its canine nickname. One of the first white settlers to come to the area—on foot—was a woman aptly named Mrs. Bassett, who decided to earn a living by providing the lonely miner with man's best friend. She became famous as a dog breeder. Later citizens changed the name to Magalia, Italian for "cottages."

Magalia, now a fast growing community, can be reached by traveling the Skyway, between Paradise and Stirling City. Like Paradise, Magalia has become a popular retirement community.

Magalia, circa 1910. The first building on the right is still standing today. The last building on the right today is the Magalia Market and Saloon, in the old historic section of town. Courtesy Jon Kitchen, and Meriam Library, California State University, Chico, Special Collections. (SC 8846)

Magalia Mine crew in front of the shaft house, circa 1898. The 7th man from the right is George Hupp; the others are unidentified. Courtesy Meriam Library, California State University, Chico, Special Collections. (SC 9805)

The "largest gold nugget in the world" was sluiced out at the Willard Mine in Magalia in April 1859. It weighed 54 pounds, and started a small Gold Rush in the town. At today's prices it would be worth about $350,000.

Supplies in the 1850s were costly. A letter from Marysville to Magalia cost around $2 postage, and took up to three weeks for delivery. The ridge today has become a thriving settlement of almost ten thousand people.

Opposite: Stirling City in winter, circa 1903. In early days the snow would entomb the area so heavily that sleds had to be used to deliver the mail to the residents. The first building on the left is the Stirling City Hotel. Today it is a Bed and Breakfast Inn, still going by the same name. Courtesy John Nopel and Meriam Library, California State University, Chico, Special Collections. (SC 11508)

STIRLING CITY

STIRLING CITY was a company town built by the Diamond Match Lumber Mill, on the ridge between Magalia and Inskip. The town is thought to have got its name from the two boilers in the sawmill, manufactured by the Stirling City Consolidated Boiler Co. In 1857 the first stage coach to cross the Sierra Nevada Mountains took the trail through this area. The Inskip Hotel, built in 1856 by John Stokes, was called Kelly and Co. When the hotel was rebuilt after burning, it was renamed Inskip, and now is listed on the National Register of Historic Places. It is the oldest building in Butte County.

Logging train, locomotive #5, Kimshew logging road near Stirling City, circa 1910.
Courtesy Meriam Library, California State University, Chico, Special Collection. (SC 7662)

STIRLING CITY RESOURCES
Inskip Inn - P.O. Box 68, Stirling City, CA 95978, (916) 873-0804
Stirling City Hotel - 16975 Skyway, (916) 873-0858

FOREST RANCH

FOREST RANCH, on Highway 32 east of Chico, is high enough to enjoy both winter snow and cool summer breezes. This mountain community of about 2,500 rests on the ridge supporting Paradise, Magalia and other Sierra Nevada towns.

Forest Ranch was once a stagecoach stop, run by a Captain Morrison, along the toll road built by the Chico and Humboldt Wagon Company in the 1860s. In the early days of 1864 and 1865, the scenic hamlet bore such names as Saunders' or Sandy's Corral. Finally, after a hotel was built to accommodate travelers, and saw mills began to thrive, people began to settle in the little alpine holding. In 1878 a Post Office was established, and the following year the Forest School was organized. Local historians think that Forest Ranch took its name from the school district.

Stage coach loaded with passengers on the old Chico-Humboldt Wagon Road, circa 1903.
The woman in front, far right, is Clara Lucas, teacher at Forest Ranch School.
Courtesy Meriam Library, California State University, Chico, Special Collections. (SC 10373)

FEATHER RIVER CANYON

James P. Beckwourth, son of a black woman and a southern plantation man, led an amazing life as a mountain man and fur trapper before he came to California around 1840. He scouted a wagon trail through the Sierra Nevada Range from Reno to Oroville. The route, still called Beckwourth's Pass, became the main east-west gateway through the northern Sierras. The town of Marysville celebrates annually the man and his contributions during Beckwourth Western Days, a kind of living museum. Courtesy of Butte County Historical Society, Oroville, California State Library and Meriam Library, California State University, Chico, Special Collection. (SC 16802)

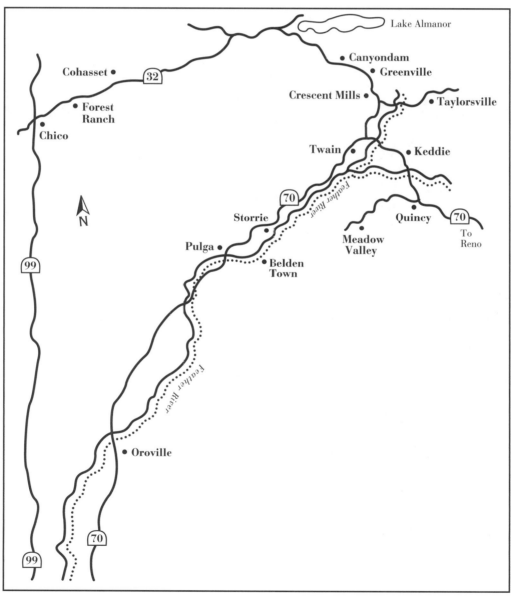

BELDEN TOWN & TWAIN

In 1817 Explorer Captain Luis Argüello led his party through the Feather River Canyon and saw what appeared to be feathers floating on the water. He called it "Rio de las Plumas" (The River of Feathers). What the Captain probably saw was feathery seeds from the willow trees along the river's edge. Arguello couldn't have imagined what importance the river would have in California's rich history. The Feather River not only gave up a fortune in gold, it also has been an invaluable source of hydroelectric power.

Highway 70 north from Oroville leads through the majestic Canyon, following the winding river and traveling through several tunnels that prison convicts cut through massive mountains of solid granite. Belden Town, with 230 residents, is the first major rest stop, with recreation and picnic areas. At Long Bar, the Belden family mine was in operation up to the turn of the century, when the Western Pacific Railroad was built. More than 250,000 ounces of gold was taken from the river itself near this canyon settlement between 1849 and 1852. Today the river's banks still offer the challenge of gold panning, and some of the best rainbow trout fishing in the state.

Bridge and train trestle at the Pulga turnoff. In 1932 the bridge was completed after three and a half years of construction. This astounding steel arch is 200 feet above the river and 680 feet long, and is banked with a curve. Courtesy John Gentles, photographer.

Belden Town Resort area. Sandy Shepherd, photographer.

BELDEN TOWN & TWAIN RESOURCES

Belden Town - (916) 283-2906, RV camp ground, picnic area, fishing

Twain - (916) 283-2130, general store, post office, gold panning

James Lee Campground - 5 miles south of Belden

Yellow Creek Trail - A two-hour hike into box canyon beginning at the rest area across from Belden Resort on Highway 70

Chambers Creek Trail - Begins off Highway 70 across from James Lee Campground 5 miles south of Belden

The Pacific Crest Trail - Accessed in Belden off Highway 70, (916) 283-2050

TWAIN LIES several miles north on the spectacular canyon drive. Until 1935, many of the little pocketed communities in the canyon had very little transportation to other areas, since trains did not stop in the small towns. For many canyon residents the Oroville-Quincy and Belden-to-Longview Stagecoach Lines were the only links to the outside world. When the highway was completed in 1935, it opened the breathtaking canyon to tourists and mountain residents alike. The railroad, built some 50 years before, was a tremendous achievement for that time. Chinese laborers built the roadbed, using only hand tools. Many of them died as a result of poor shelter and clothing, extremes of weather and exceptionally hard physical labor.

The famous Rich Bar, described in Dame Shirley's letters about northern mining towns, lies on the river between Belden and Twain. Rich Bar got its name from a strike which yielded some $3 million in gold.

The Western Pacific Railroad became the nation's sixth transcontinental railroad upon its completion in 1909, winding through the Feather River Canyon and over the Sierra summit, following much of Beckwourth's trail. Plumas County surveyor Arthur W. Keddie, for whom the railroad camp of Keddie was named, had had a dream for such a plan since the mid 1860s. As giant railroad companies like Southern Pacific, Union Pacific and Denver and Rio Grande Western changed control, the dream for a railroad to link Salt Lake City and San Francisco took many turns and setbacks. Once George Gould, owner of the DRGW decided to build his own railroad to the Pacific, absolute secrecy was imposed. Men posing as miners were sent into the Feather River Canyon country to stake out mining claims and survey the area. In 1903 the Western Pacific Railroad was incorporated and in 1905 it was announced that

Western Pacific would link up with the DRGW to provide a competing route to the east. On November 1, 1909, two railroad crews met at the Spanish Creek Bridge near Keddie and joined the last link in the steel ribbon connecting Salt Lake to Oakland. In the 1930s a split was added to the tracks, allowing for a northward route to Klamath Falls, Oregon; however, the switch to access the northern leg was not installed until diesel engines were put in use in 1953. In 1949, a reenactment of the final spike being driven home was held at the same bridge near Keddie, accompanied by the "Old '49" engine that pulled the first passenger train through the canyon in 1910, a California Zephyr, and the "Jupiter" of the Virginia City and Truckee Railroad. Portola, a lumber town east of Quincy, has become one of the main railroad centers, and celebrates annually the rich railroad tradition with Railroad Days.

The railroad tracks split into two directions near Keddie at the Spanish Creek Bridge, site of the final link-up of the railroad coming from the east. The split tracks lead to the north to connect with the Great Northern Railroad, or to the east, toward Portola and on to Utah. Courtesy of John Gentles, photographer.

QUINCY

THE ROUTE to Quincy, Highway 70, is a 50-mile serpentine path following the Feather River through breathtaking scenery: gorgeous seasonal colors, splashing waterfalls, a raging river, impressive water power plants, and freight trains inching around the mountain's curves. Quincy is just the beginning. Plumas County offers historic buildings, beautiful lakes, prime fishing spots, winter sports, and hiking trails to explore.

Quincy, home to 4,271 people, is a quaint town in a small valley that appears to have been carved right out of the mountains. It can be reached from Highway 70 out of Marysville, Highway 395 north of Reno and west from nearby Portola, or even Highway 32 east of Chico and connecting with Highway 89. Quincy is the county seat for Plumas County and the major shopping center for many surrounding mountain settlements. It has new and modern business buildings as well as well-kept historical landmarks.

As more pioneers came to California seeking gold, timber became more and more valuable. The mining camps constantly needed more lumber as boom towns began to explode. In the American Valley, near the present town of Quincy, a sawmill was built in 1852 by three men named Cate, Judkings, and Boyington. Sawmills sprouted up all over the mountains, which were carpeted with pine trees as a far as the eye could see. Oxen and horses pulled the huge logs to the sawmills to be cut for shipping.

When cutting up a log for lumber, virtually the entire of log is utilized. Mulch and fuel are made from the tree's bark. The rounded sides of the log, edgings, and trim ends go in to the chipper for particle board. The outer part of the log, with the fewest knots, is cut into boards or planks of various thicknesses. As the knots increase towards the center of the log, heavier planks or beams are sawed from these sections. The center of the log, the oldest part of the tree where most of the knots are located, is used for structural beams that are very strong and not weakened by knots.

Fourth of July parade in Quincy on Main Street, circa 1900.
Courtesy Plumas County Museum, Quincy.

Log wagon on Main Street in Quincy, circa 1890. Courtesy Plumas County Museum, Quincy.

Quincy school, built in 1876 for $4,000. This building was replaced in 1905 by the present building. Courtesy of Plumas County Museum, Quincy.

Quincy Schoolhouse, built 1905, shown after a heavy snowstorm in 1992 that helped to end the six-and-a-half year drought in California. Courtesy Jerry Cooper, photographer.

QUINCY RESOURCES

POINTS OF INTEREST
Feather River Junior College
Plumas County Museum - 500 Jackson Street
Portola's Railroad Museum - (916) 832-4131
Bucks Lake - Bucks Lake Road, southwest of Quincy
Site of The Plumas House - SW corner of Main and Bucks Lake Roads
Site of American Ranch and Hotel -355 Main Street
Pioneer School House - Plumas County Fairgrounds
Plumas Eureka State Park - Various hiking and skiing trails
The Pacific Crest Trail - On the Quincy-La Porte Road, south of Quincy (916) 283-2050

FESTIVALS & EVENTS
Plumas County Fair - Second weekend in August
Railroad Days - Portola. Contact the Eastern Plumas Chamber of Commerce
Winter Fest - Chester, in January, contact Chester\Lake Almanor Chamber of Commerce
Old Time Fiddling Championship - Quincy, in July
Northern Sierra Indian Days - Third weekend in September, (916) 283-3402
Mountain Harvest Festival
A Taste of Quincy - Second weekend in October, (916) 283-0188

BED AND BREAKFAST INNS & LODGES
The Feather Bed - 542 Jackson Street, (916) 283-0102
Greenhorn Creek Guest Ranch - (916) 283-0930
Gray Eagle Lodge - P.O. Box 38, Blairsden, Ca. 96103 (916) 836-2511 or 1-800-635-8778 (No. Cal.)
Bucks Lake Lodge - (916) 283-2333
Bucks Lakeshore Resort - (916) 283-6900

CAMPGROUNDS & RV PARKS
Grizzly Creek - (916) 534-6500   Lower Bucks - (916) 534-6500
Snake Lake - (916) 283-0555   Sundew - (916) 534-6500
Mill Creek - (916) 534-6500   White Horse - (916) 534-6500
Silver Lake - (916) 283-0555   Deanes Valley - (916) 283-0555
Motel & Trailer Park - (916) 283-1765

MEADOW VALLEY

MEADOW VALLEY, between Quincy and Bucks Lake, is surrounded by towering pine trees and green meadows. Spanish Creek meanders through the lush valley. Like many other settlements in the mountains, Meadow Valley got its foothold in the lumbering industry. The neighboring community of Spanish Ranch began when two Mexican men came to the area searching for gold and stayed on to raise beef and board the miners' pack animals. A Post Office was established in Meadow Valley, then transferred to Spanish Ranch, only to be moved back again in 1864, when Quincy's Post Office was founded. Before that the mail came out of Bidwell Bar, and was delivered only once a week during the winter months. St. Bernard and New-foundland dogs, pulling sleds weighing up to 600 pounds, were used to carry the mail until horse snowshoes were introduced in the winter of 1865.

Meadow Valley Hotel, pre-1890. A legend on the back of the photograph identifies some of the people: Thomas and Lizzie Hughes are the 6th and 7th people from the left in the center. Frank Hill is the 9th person from the left and James Mumford is on the extreme right. Courtesy Plumas County Museum, Quincy.

Schools in the mountain area were real treasures, for qualified teachers were not always readily available. Meadow Valley School, circa 1905. Hay Moon, left front row, and Fong Moon to his right.

Taylorsville School, circa 1889. Both photos courtesy Plumas County Museum, Quincy.

TAYLORSVILLE

TAYLORSVILLE, about 12 miles from Greenville off Highway 89 turnoff, was named for the first settler, Jobe T. Taylor, who built a flour mill in 1852. Taylorsville fully enjoys all four seasons, with beautiful fall colors, crystal white snow drifts, lush green meadows and gentle warm summer breezes. Mt. Hough, looming in the background, has become a popular spot for hang gliding enthusiasts and a unique area for rockhounds to find fossils and arrowheads.

Taylorsville, Plumas County, circa 1870. North side of Main street, looking east. Vernon House is on the far left. Courtesy Meriam Library, California State University, Chico, Special Collections. (SC 9465)

TAYLORSVILLE RESOURCES

Taylorsville Museum - April to October (916) 284-6600
Antelope Lake and Campgrounds - Call Chamber of Commerce
Indian Creek Campgrounds - Call Chamber of Commerce
Lone Rock Campground- Call Chamber of Commerce
Silver Buckle Rodeo - July 4 - (916 283-6345 or 1-800-326-2247
Plumas County Chamber of Commerce - (916) 283-2045 or 1-800-326-2247
Antelope Lake Nature Trail - One and a half mile walk, access next to Lone Rock Campground

CRESCENT MILLS

As THE SEARCH for gold spread up through the Sierra Nevada Range and the Feather River Canyon, lumber was in high demand for building wing-dams and water flumes. As mountain settlements and lumber camps sprang up among the hills, even more lumber was needed for houses, schools, stores and churches.

Crescent Mills, once a thriving lumber town, is located in Indian Valley, about ten miles east of Greenville, surrounded by tall pines and numerous waterways.

With only 665 residents, Crescent Mills is a very small town, completely dependent on the town's lumber mill and tourist trade. This Indian Valley country is incomparably beautiful, with masses of golden oak, chokecherry and dogwood trees watered by crystalline streams.

Crescent Mills, Plumas County, circa 1890. Courtesy Meriam Library, California State University Chico, Special Collections. (SC 9450)

CRESCENT MILLS RESOURCE
Crescent Mills Bed and Breakfast Inn - (916) 284-9905

Green Mountain Mine at Crescent Mills, circa 1880. Courtesy Plumas County Museum, Quincy.

Logging crew or railroad crew in Plumas County along the Feather River. This undated picture, entitled "The Whole Dam Crew," shows Truman Wright, third from the left. Courtesy Community Memorial Museum, Yuba City.

GREENVILLE

ONE OF THE MOST spectacular drives is along Highway 89 near its intersection with Highway 70. Heading toward Greenville and Lake Almanor on Highway 89, the road follows Indian Creek, around mountains of tall pine trees and through the lush green meadows of Indian Valley. Mt. Hough rises in splendor as the road nears the historic logging and mining town of Greenville, which is larger than the previous towns on this route.

Greenville has achieved a unique blend of historic buildings, mountain style structures and a few modern stores and homes. Today the town, with a population of 1,396, exudes an overwhelming feeling of peace and quiet against a background of awesome scenery.

Greenville, Main Street, circa 1920. First building on the left is thought to still be standing in a remodeled state. The fourth building on the left serves as a hardware store today. The first building on the right also still stands. Courtesy Plumas County Museum, Quincy.

GREENVILLE RESOURCES

Round Valley Reservoir - Great bird watching area - (916) 284-6542
Butt Lake - Prattville turnoff
Indian Falls Trail - 1/2 mile (steep) excursion with waterfalls Indian
   Falls Road, off Highway 89 southeast of Greenville
Round Valley Lake Nature Walk - 3 miles from Greenville on the
   Greenville-Round Valley Road
Digger Moore's Sierra Lodge - (916) 284-6565
Hideaway Resort Motel - (916) 284-7915
Golddigger Days -Third weekend in July (916) 284-6633

Opposite, top: Greenville Harness Shop, circa 1890. Courtesy Plumas County Museum, Quincy.

Opposite, below: Greenville Indian Boarding School, circa 1894. Edward Ament and his wife were the teachers. A variety of ethnic groups attended this school. Courtesy Special Collections, Meriam Library, California State University, Chico. (SC 8590)

CANYONDAM & PRATTVILLE

CANYONDAM, a very small mountain town with only 86 residents, sits at the south end of Lake Almanor, the largest lake in Plumas County. One could easily call this "God's Country," with its close proximity to Butt Lake and Lassen Volcanic National Park, and its grand view of Mt. Lassen. The Pacific Crest National Trail (PCT), 2,600 miles from Canada to Mexico, passes through Plumas County for 80 scenic miles.

Prattville, a tiny mountain village tucked among the pine-scented Sierras, is reached by traveling further west around the lower end of Lake Almanor, a few miles from Canyondam. This country is a part of the Caribou Wilderness Area.

The pioneers who came here in search of gold and stayed to build the surviving lumber towns are regarded as heroes. But the Indians, long before the white man, came, lived as one with the land. One can only hope that present and future generations will preserve the beautiful country near Lake Almanor, as did the wise Native Americans.

Prattville, near Canyondam in Plumas County, circa 1905. Courtesy Meriam Library, California State University, Chico, Special Collections. (SC 2820)

CANYONDAM RESOURCES

Lake Almanor - Intersection of Highways 89, 36 and 147
Butt Valley Reservoir - 5 miles south of Highway 89, opposite Prattville turnoff

---

THE LOST SIERRAS

Butte County Pine and Hardwood Lumber Co. near Clipper Mills, hauling logs with their steam tractor. Courtesy California Room, Yuba County Library, Marysville.

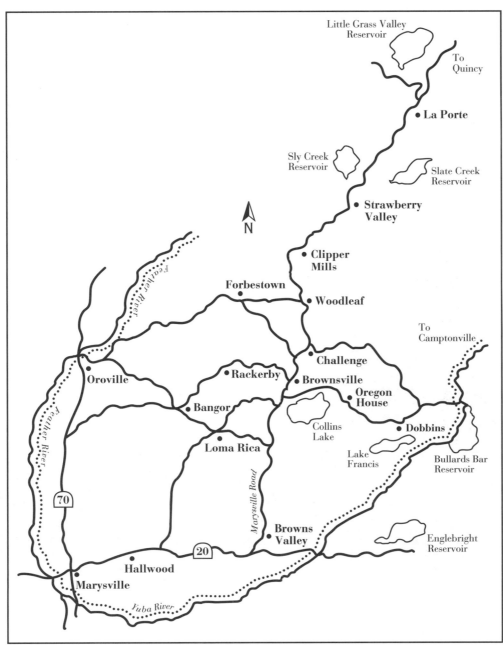

BROWNS VALLEY

BROWNS VALLEY sits in the foothills about 12 miles east of Marysville, at the junction of Highway 20 and Marysville–La Porte Road. This crossroads was an early stagecoach stop, sporting some 5 hotels and 24 saloons. Later large freight trains, often called "prairie schooners", came up from Marysville with enormous loads of supplies destined for the mines and lumber camps in the high country. The Flag Mine, the Jefferson Mine, the Pennsylvania Mine and the Sweet Vengeance Mine, among others, gave employment to a large number of men in the Browns Valley countryside. In 1851 the first stamp mill for crushing gold-bearing quartz was built in this little town. Today, with 3000 residents, the town is growing fast, attracting many new families to its scenic hillside.

School in Browns Valley District, late 1800s. Courtesy Community Memorial Museum, Yuba City.

BROWNS VALLEY RESOURCES

Fletcher's Tuff Stuff Jerky - (916) 741-1417, 7155 Marysville Road
Collins Lake Recreation Area - (916) 692-1600
Sycamore Recreation - (916) 743-7959

Browns Valley Store, with a 12-mule team carrying the mail, 1890s. Courtesy Yuba Feather Historical Association, Forbestown.

Left: Edwin A. Forbes, Marysville District Attorney in the 1880s, grew up between Oregon House and Dobbins. He was a crack target shooter, breaking the world's record, a Major in the California U.S. Volunteers, and Adjutant General of California, as well as a teacher and later an attorney. Courtesy California Room, Yuba County Library, Marysville.

DOBBINS

DOBBINS, once only a large ranch at the end of the wagon trail, now is a bustling little mountain community neighboring two beautiful lakes. The ranch on Dobbins Creek was established by brothers William and Mark Dobbins in 1849.

Lake Francis, formed from the damming of Dobbins Creek, and Bullards Bar Reservoir are close at hand. Bullards Bar Dam, the highest concrete-arch dam in California, supplies water for the P.G.& E. powerplants below.

DOBBINS RESOURCES

Emerald Cove Resort & Marina - (Bullards Bar) -(916) 692-2166
Bullards Bar Reservoir - Outdoor sports and camping
Historic Sacred Heart Catholic Church

Dobbins Hotel, circa 1920. Owner Joseph Merriam was one of Yuba County's pioneer hotel men. Courtesy California Room, Yuba County Library, Marysville.

OREGON HOUSE

OREGON HOUSE, on the road to Camptonville, once was considered to be the party town of the hills. It boasted of having sold some 250 tickets to a grand ball in 1853, said to be the first big party in the hills. Settled by Larry Young in 1850, the town began to develop as a thriving settlement in 1852 when it became a popular rest stop for the mule trains heading up the mountain with supplies. Oregon House school was the second school to be built in Yuba County, in 1854, and for years was considered to be the best. Today Oregon House is a quiet hamlet tucked away among the pines near Collins Lake, the home of a winery and a museum run by the Fellowship of Friends.

Nearby another historic town known as Frenchtown was founded by a man named Paul Vavasseur, who was of French descent. Today it is not much more than a memory, with only a few landmarks to verify its existence

Oregon House lies in a small valley between rolling hills. With its moderate climate and open terrain, the area is ideal for raising cattle, as well as various types of produce. The town's small Post Office, down the road a bit from its old location at the two-story hotel and stage stop, boasts of being the first Post Office in California to go first class. In 1983 the Post Office claimed to serve some 300 families, and ten years later the population has grown only slightly.

Oregon House Hotel, built in 1852, and Post Office with the Postmaster, Clara Phelan (left) and her family posed on steps, circa 1897. Courtesy Jim Morgan.

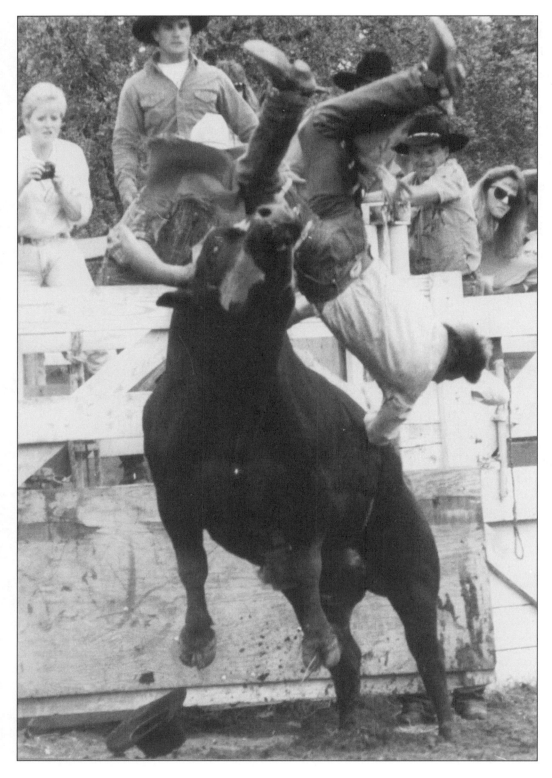

Oregon House Rodeo bull riding event, 1990. Courtesy Jerry Cooper.

OREGON HOUSE RESOURCES

Old Frenchtown Adobe - Built in the 1850s by French settlers on Frenchtown Road north of Oregon House.
Old Oregon House School - Now the Community Center, corner Rice's Crossing and Texas Hill Roads
Museum of Classical Chinese Furniture - 12585 Rice's Crossing Road, (916) 692-2244
Renaissance Vineyards And Winery - 12585 Rice's Crossing Road, (916) 692-2222
Oregon House Rodeo - April, (916) 692-1000
Cabin Fever Spaghetti Feed - Last Saturday in February
Oktoberfest - Second weekend in October, call Lion's Club

RACKERBY

IN ITS EARLY HISTORY the mining town of Rackerby could not make up its mind on a name. It was called Hansonville, Miller's Ranch, and Paulineville before the name of Rackerby finally stuck.

Rackerby can be reached by several roads leading from neighboring Brownsville, from Marysville's outlying community of Loma Rica, or from Bangor. Like many other old mining camps, this settlement once flourished, but now sits small and quiet, reflecting on a glorious past.

In 1851 the population of some 1000 worked in the local mines. Most of today's 500 residents travel elsewhere for work, but find this foothill community a fine place to be a modern-day pioneer or woodsman or even gold miner.

William and Ruth Rackerby with their children in front of the general store, Rackerby's Camp, which also housed the Post Office and "The Red House," circa 1892.
Courtesy Yuba Feather Historical Association, Forbestown.

Rackerby Hotel and Stage, circa 1900. Courtesy Yuba Feather Historical Association, Forbestown.

Napoleon B. Abbott, early 1900s. Mr. Abbott peddled fruit and vegetables in the mountain area now often referred to as the Lost Sierras. The photograph was taken near Rackerby. Courtesy Yuba Feather Historical Association, Forbestown.

BROWNSVILLE

BROWNSVILLE, one of the larger towns of the Lost Sierras, attracts both retired people and many new families. Striving to bring in new commerce and recreation, this picturesque village abounds with inviting tree-lined lanes leading to fine, well-kept homes, especially beautiful in autumn, when the leaves are in full color.

The town was named for Isaac E. Brown, who built the town's first sawmill in 1851. A hotel was built in 1855 to accommodate the growing number of travelers through the Sierra high country. The community itself was not established until the late 1870s when a general store, a Wells Fargo office, an I.O.O.F. Hall and a private school were in operation, with a resident population of 100.

Freight wagons pulled by four to ten horses often passed through town, the skilled driver often using a "jerk line" to maneuver his team and cargo over the steep, winding trails. Drivers changed their exhausted horses for fresh teams at many of the mountain stops.

Right: Brownsville Meat Market truck with J. Wallnett, proprietor. Courtesy Yuba Feather Historical Association. Forbestown.

A "freight train" stops at Brownsville, circa 1890. Courtesy Yuba Feather Historical Association, Forbestown.

An ox-team was used to haul logs at Sharon Valley, near Brownsville, circa 1883. The V-flume transported lumber to Honcut, outside of Oroville. Courtesy Yuba Feather Historical Association, Forbestown.

Sharon Valley, near Brownsville, had a fine hotel to serve workers at several thriving sawmills in the vicinity. The oxen rest from their labor, while a sturdy horse is hitched to a slick new buggy. Courtesy Yuba Feather Historical Association, Forbestown.

A vintage logging truck stops in front of Sharon Valley Hotel, also known as the Crane, circa 1915. The men are Marcio Weiss (left) and Eddy Leel.

Squire Sawmill, at nearby Gibsonville, 1860s. Both photos courtesy Yuba Feather Historical Association, Forbestown.

Brownsville Store, Post Office and omnibus, circa 1915. Courtesy Yuba Feather Historical Association, Forbestown.

BROWNSVILLE RESOURCES

POINTS OF INTEREST
Brownsville Aero Pines Airport - 8487 La Porte Road, (916) 675-2321
Antique Shops
C & R Dragon Fly Gifts - 9042 La Porte Road
Mary's Country Store & Gifts - La Porte Road
Mountain Seasons Inn and Gifts & Antiques - (916) 675-2180
Lost Sierra Association - Tourist information, P.O. Box 728, Brownsville,
  Ca. 95919 (916) 675-1225
Lottie Brennan's (Knoxdale Institute) - Built in 1878 as a girls' finishing
  school, the second one west of the Mississippi. Today it is a lovely
  restaurant. (916) 675-1003

FESTIVALS & EVENTS
Mountain Fair - July 4th weekend, (916) 675-1225
Annual Logging Olympics - At Mountain Fair

LODGING & CAMPGROUNDS
Mountain Seasons Inn - La Porte Rd. (916) 675-2180
Collins Lake Recreation Area - (near Oregon House) Marysville Road,
  (916) 692-1600

BROWNSVILLE not only preserves its mining and lumbering history, but continues to be the major link between different mountain areas. Today, with a population of over 6,000, the town offers lodging, medical facilities, banks, and a variety of commerce, as well as an airport for small aircraft.

FORBESTOWN

BUSTLING LITTLE Forbestown is unique in that it lies in both Butte and Yuba Counties, on the Challenge - Forbestown Cutoff Road between Oroville and Brownsville. Forbestown, named for several Forbes brothers, boasted over 3,000 residents during the gold mining boom. It was the second largest town in Butte County in 1853.

FORBESTOWN RESOURCES

Yuba Feather Pioneer Museum - New York Flat Road
Forbestown Historic School House - Next to the Museum
Masonic Hall - Built in 1855
Rustic Buckhorn Saloon - Forbestown Road
S.E.B. Ranch - (916) 675-2082, September - October, apples
Lost Sierra Association - Tourist information, P.O. Box 728, Brownsville, Ca. 95919 (916) 675-1225

Forbestown, winter of 1900. Courtesy Yuba Feather Historical Association, Forbestown.

CHALLENGE

CHALLENGE, a tiny mountain retreat, population 300, nestled among the pines and babbling brooks, straddles the Marysville–La Porte Road. It is situated between Brownsville and Clipper Mills on the road to Woodleaf resort and historic La Porte. Challenge Mills, as it was known in earlier days, was a mill compound owned by A.M. Leach in 1874. As Leach's mill grew, he built a railroad through the forest to transport logs to his mill. Parts of the trestle and railroad ties can still be seen today. During those prosperous times he also built a thirty-mile-long water-filled V-flume to Honcut, using some 135,000 board feet for each mile, in order to provide a quicker means of transporting his logs to a big pond near the Honcut railroad. After the lumber operations were gone, the community dwindled down to only a wide spot in the road, but oh, how lovely that little spot remains.

Challenge School, circa 1910. The children appear to be dressed in their Sunday hats for some special occasion. Courtesy California Room, Yuba County Library, Marysville.

The Leach narrow gauge logging train ran from Challenge to Beanville, circa 1890. When Leach opened another sawmill in Woodville, later known as Woodleaf, he extended the line to the new mill. Courtesy Yuba Feather Historical Association, Forbestown.

Dr. Geerheart of Challenge made house calls with his horse and buggy in early 1900s.

Challenge Hotel (once known as the Ribble Hotel), circa 1890. The Challenge Hotel, built in 1886, gave a big dance each New Years Eve, drawing crowds from the surrounding communities as well as Marysville. The hotel burned in 1914, but had stood for 28 years near the west end of the present U.S. Forest Service Rangers Station.
Both photographs courtesy Yuba Feather Historical Association, Forbestown.

WOODLEAF

THIS UNIQUE COLONY was founded in 1859 by Charles Barker and was then known as Barker's Ranch. For its 140 years of existence, Wood-leaf, for the most part, has been an undivided piece of land encompassing 185 acres. It started out as only a store and rooming house, but later was transformed into a luxury hotel with Persian rugs, velvet drapes and mahogany furniture. The brick Woodville House, built by James Wood, was a popular over-night stop for such people as Lotta Crab-tree, Ulysses S. Grant, and Black Bart, the gentleman bandit, who was courting a local girl. John C. Falck purchased Woodville in 1878 for $4,000. In 1942 the land was sold, but two small parcels with private residences remained in the Falck family.

Today Woodleaf is a non-profit Christian organization for youth in the summer and an outdoor educational site during the other months. In 1968 and 1972 the Young Life Organ-ization purchased back the two small parcels, reuniting the original piece of land.

Woodleaf Lodge, 1860s. Courtesy Yuba Feather Historical Association, Forbestown.

Woodleaf Lodge; Bill Lang sitting in his car, circa 1915. Courtesy Yuba-Feather Historical Association, Forbestown.

CLIPPER MILLS

THE FIRST water-powered sawmill, the Pine Grove Mill, was built in 1852. In 1855 and 1856, the Clipper Mill was built by A.P. Willey and Elisha Scott, but was later bought by Union Lumber Co. It is said that Clipper Mills got its name because some of the sawmill machinery was brought around the Horn on a clipper ship.

Clipper Mills, circa 1890. Pictured is one of two steam tractors used by Union Lumber Company. One tractor worked in the woods while the other hauled the lumber to Oroville. Courtesy Yuba Feather Historical Association.

Clipper Mills sawmill on a busy Sunday morning, circa 1865. Courtesy Yuba Feather Historical Association, Forbestown.

STRAWBERRY VALLEY

Strawberry Valley, high in the Sierras, is 43 miles northeast of Marysville on the road to La Porte. Once a thriving lumbering and mining center, now the little mountain valley is a resort for fishing and camping. The Soaper-Wheeler Company, a tree farming enterprise in operation in Strawberry Valley since 1904, once owned a thriving sawmill. It is best known today for reforestation. In May 1973 the company held a huge celebration when their 1,000,000th tree was planted by Nancy Reagan, at that time first lady of California.

No one is certain just how Strawberry Valley got its name, whether from wild berries growing in the area or, according to an old-time tale, from two early miners called "Straw" and "Berry."

William and Addie Tompkins, owners of the North Star Hotel, north of Strawberry Valley, circa 1890. Courtesy Yuba-Feather Historical Association, Forbestown.

The famous North Star Hotel and stage stop, circa 1890. Courtesy Yuba-Feather Historical Association, Forbestown.

The Leach lumber flume crosses Owl Gulch east of Strawberry Valley, circa 1888. This amazing structure was only a part of the 30-mile flume, built during a time when nothing, apparently, was impossible. Courtesy Yuba-Feather Historical Association, Forbestown.

Dave Hall used his "Snowbird" to haul mail, packages and sometimes passengers in the winter between Strawberry Valley and La Porte, circa 1950. The propeller drove the cockpit forward, resting on three skis. This mode of transportation was short-lived, as it was very expensive to operate. Courtesy Yuba Feather Historical Association, Forbestown.

LA PORTE

THE TOWN WAS NAMED after La Porte, Indiana, in 1857 by a local banker, Frank Everets. Earlier the mining camp had the name of Rabbit Creek for the snowshoe rabbits often seen in the vicinity. When the Post Office tried to name the town Rabbit Town, residents became highly indignant.

La Porte, at 5,000 feet elevation, is an old gold mining town that yielded $60 million in gold between 1855 and 1871 from hydraulic mining. The main road is the Marysville–La Porte Road off Highway 20, open all year. During the summer months only, a 30-mile dirt road connects the little town with the county seat, Quincy.

La Porte was the birthplace of world-wide competitive skiing. In 1867, the Alturas Snowshoe Club held the first recognized tournament, with competitors from European countries. At that time the skiers used almost unimaginable 12-foot-long boards for skis.

La Porte, March 1911. Courtesy Community Memorial Museum, Yuba City.

Horses and men work together to haul a boiler down main street, La Porte, circa 1880.
Courtesy Plumas County Museum, Quincy.

The Marysville –La Porte Stage, 1900 - 1911. Holding the reins is Mrs. Ed Pike. Left rear man is J.V. Parks.
Driver is M. Bustillos. A close inspection reveals snowshoes on the horses.
Courtesy Plumas County Museum, Quincy.

Dominic Rickey's Crew at Slate Creek, near La Porte, circa 1916. Courtesy Plumas County Museum, Quincy.

LA PORTE RESOURCES

POINTS OF INTEREST
St. Croix Sculpture Art Gallery - (916) 675-0707
Union Hotel - (916) 675-2525, World's first Ski Hostel
Marty's Place - (916) 675-2753, gold and gifts
Sarsaparilla Palace - A Historic Site and Mine Museum, (916) 675-2753

LODGING
Gold Country Lodge - (916) 675-2322
Union Hotel - (916) 675-2525

CAMPGROUNDS & RV PARKS
Little Grass Valley Reservoir
Sly Creek Reservoir - Camping, fishing and canoeing
Slate Creek Reservoir - Camping, fishing
Black Rock, Little Beaver, Peninsula, Red Feather, and Running Deer
  Campgrounds - (916) 675-2462

THE GOLD COUNTRY

A three-stamp mill used to crush gold-bearing ore at Washington's Red Ledge Mine. This mill was donated to the city of Grass Valley in memory of the "Cousin Jacks" and stands in the center of town. "Cousin Jack" was the nickname given to the Cornish miners brought in to the area to help with hard-rock mining.
Sandra Shepherd, photographer.

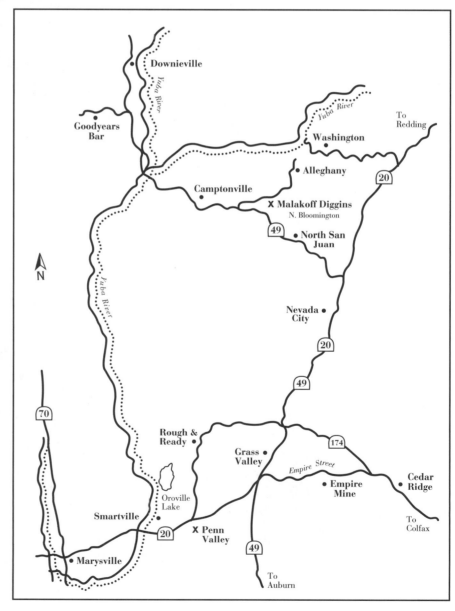

TIMBUCTOO

In 1865, TIMBUCTOO was the largest town in Eastern Yuba County, with about forty stores, hotels, saloons, a church, a theater and 2,000 residents. The town's name came about when a black miner found a very rich deposit. As the news traveled along the Yuba River, people began to tag the area with the name of the miner's hometown in Africa (Timbuktu). Timbuctoo and the neighboring town of Smartville grew when hydraulic mining companies came to wash away the surrounding mountainsides. Evidence of this can still be seen today. As debris from the hydraulic mining covered the little mining sites along the Yuba River, such places as Rose Bar and Saw-Mill Bar became extinct, and the miners and residents moved to the newer, thriving areas. Today, with fewer than 50 residents, Timbuctoo is not much more than a ghost town struggling to remain a colorful memory and historic landmark.

The Wells Fargo Office in Timbuctoo was not only the bank, but also the stop for the short-lived Pony Express run. Only the cornerstones remain today. Courtesy California Room, Yuba County Library, Marysville.

Timbuctoo in a very early photograph, probably from the 1850s. Today it is almost a ghost town. Courtesy California Room, Yuba County Library, Marysville.

146

SMARTVILLE

SMARTVILLE was named after James Smart, who built a hotel in the area near the larger town of Timbuctoo. Many mining camps and towns were destroyed or covered over by hydraulic mining. Parks Bar, one such place, is at the site where the Highway 20 bridge crosses the Yuba River.

Smartville grew as a result of the profitable hydraulic mining until the Sawyer Decision was passed in 1884 prohibiting the dumping of debris in rivers. Prior to the passing of the landmark law, farmlands downstream were being destroyed, mining camps were being covered with mud, and the riverbeds were raised as much as seventy-five feet in some areas. It is estimated that between 1849 and 1914 some 1,146,000,000 cubic yards of mining debris flowed down toward San Francisco Bay, with 333,000,000 cubic yards of debris in the Yuba River alone.

Today Smartville, like Timbuctoo, gives the visitor a feeling of stepping back in time. The little foothill town lies along the banks of the Yuba River, among oak studded hillsides, and along the narrow winding road that once served as a stagecoach route. Smartville and several neighboring communities are beginning to grow as more people want to leave the crowded cities for the open countryside of Northern California.

A very early photograph shows the Parks Bar crew and camp, circa 1852. Parks Bar, named for David Parks, was the richest of all the working bars on the Yuba River. David Parks, who arrived with his wife and children in 1848, returned to the east with all the gold his family could carry. Courtesy California Room, Yuba County Library, Marysville.

Above: Smartville, circa 1914. The quiet little community was once the home of 1,500 miners, a hydraulic mining industry, 16 saloons and a church. Courtesy William Peardon, prior Postmaster and native of Smartville. The Peardon Hotel and Saloon were owned by Mr. Peardon's father.

Right: Church of Immaculate Conception, built in 1871, after the first Catholic church, built in 1852, burned down. This church, on the corner of Main and O'Brien Streets, is one of the last remaining landmarks of the town's history. Sandra Shepherd, photographer.

AFTER THE Sawyer Decision was passed, mining towns like Timbuctoo and Smartville quickly declined in population with mainly only Chinese residents remaining. A much-admired local man, James O'Brien, was honored with three Japanese Zelkova trees, given to him by the Chinese for his kindness and friendship. It is believed that these trees, of the type the Chinese use to build their temples and shrines, are today the oldest and largest of their species in America. In the 1930s, during the Depression years, many men came back to the area looking for work in the mines, agreeing to pay ten percent of their gold income to the owners. But there was no great profit to be made and the plan folded.

Inside the Peardon Saloon in Smartville, circa 1914. From left to right: Alex McPhearson, Art Johnson, John J. Murphy, unknown, Bill Peardon, Sr., Elmer Colling, Louis Harvey, Mr. Cassidy, Phil Smith, Charles Compton, Edward McGannery, Mr. Goodman, Art Spencer, and Harry Johnson.
Courtesy Bill Peardon, Jr.

SMARTVILLE RESOURCES
Historic Catholic Church
Historic Masonic Hall
Skipper Cove Campground - Mooney Flat Road

PENN VALLEY

As a stop for the freight wagon route between Sacramento and the Mother Lode country, Penn Valley was the center of an attractive, fruitful valley, referred to as the "Pantry of the Northern Mines," ideal for grazing, growing fruit and vegetables, and farming. Today, with beautiful Lake Wildwood nearby, the town is booming. Recreation includes horseback riding, fishing, boating, hunting and the all-American sport, the annual rodeo. A unique museum in the town houses a collection of artifacts from such ancient civilizations as Babylon, Mesopotamia, Carthage and Greece. This museum, a charter of the Ancient and Modern Art Museum, has relocated several times from Sacramento, Nevada City and finally to its present site. School children have taken many field trips to the display of mummies, dinosaurs, meteorites, and other curiosities. Exhibits have included ancient and modern African masks, a local artist's work and other artists' work from earlier centuries.

Penn Valley's Annual Rodeo, circa 1989. Coming out of the chute is Jerry Cooper, a Marysville Postal employee. Courtesy Jerry Cooper.

PENN VALLEY RESOURCES

Penn Valley Chamber of Commerce - (916) 432-1104
Museum of Ancient and Modern Art - 11392 Pleasant Valley Road, (916) 432-3080
Penn Valley Firemen's Association Rodeo - Last Sunday in April
Western Gateway Park - 80 acres
South Yuba River Project - (916) 273-3884, hiking, fishing and camping
Historic Bridgeport Covered Bridge - Lake Wildwood turnoff near Penn Valley. With a 225 ft. span, this is the longest single-span covered bridge in the United States.
Bridgeport - Between Highways 20 and 49, great for swimming and gold panning

ROUGH AND READY

Rough and Ready was named for Zachary Taylor, "Old Rough and Ready," and founded by miners led by A.A. Townsend in 1849. With gold fever rampant and several successful gold strikes in the area, every foot of ground was worked in search of treasure. When a mining tax was placed on each claim, the 3,000 miners of Rough and Ready demonstrated their fury by voting to secede from the Union on April 7, 1850. But the new independent state did not last long, for as soon as the Fourth of July rolled around everyone raised the nation's flag in celebration.

This unique historical mountain town has struggled to stay alive even during World War II, when the Post Office closed for five years. When it reopened, the tough little town had to fight to keep its name. The Post Office insisted that one town cannot have two names, Rough and Ready. But the the local townspeople stood their ground, and the Rough and Ready Post Office resumed operations in 1948. Just a few miles south of Grass Valley, the little town still survives, and still holds its annual Secession Day Celebration. Its unique Post Office cancellation has become a collector's item for many philatelists.

Rough and Ready, circa 1857. Courtesy California State Library, California Collection, Sacramento. (Neg. # 229)

ROUGH AND READY RESOURCES
Secession Day - Last Sunday in June
Chili Cook Off- First or second Sunday in April
Historical Buildings - W.H. Fippin Blacksmith Shop (1850), Grange Hall (1850).
Little Wedding Chapel -Weddings for couples from all over the world.

GRASS VALLEY

GRASS VALLEY, with pine-studded hillsides and many reminders of days past, lies about 30 miles east of Marysville on High 20 in Nevada County, and also on Highway 49. The town has an authentic aura of Gold Rush days. It was named when immigrants, traveling over the Sierras, found their strayed cattle resting in a beautiful "grass valley." The lush green meadows and protective hills impressed the travelers then as today. The first post office in the area was called Centerville, but it was later changed to Grass Valley.

Local lore has it that in 1850 George McKnight (or Knight according to some historians) stubbed his toe on a piece of gold-bearing quartz while out chasing his cow in the moonlight. Before long miners swarmed into the valley, which in time produced some $960 million in gold. Nevada County came to be known as the world's most productive hard-rock gold mining area. As the population grew, townspeople put up theaters, rooming houses, stores, hotels, and churches. In spite of numerous fires in the early days, many beautiful historic buildings and Victorian houses miraculously still remain standing.

In 1851, with gold mining at its peak, the population reached 20,000. Just outside of town, tunnels still bore into the earth from the Empire, the Pennsylvania, the North Star, and the Idaho-Maryland Mines. Periodically, work is resumed in the mines, but costly operation has made gold mining unprofitable today. The population has dropped to 9,048, but the town has grown by one-third since 1980, and continues to attract newcomers.

Grass Valley was once home to internationally famous celebrities. Lola Montez, baptized Maria Dolores Eliza Rosanna Gilbert, was the beautiful mistress of King Ludwig of Bavaria. Scandal followed her both in California and abroad. Miners came from miles around to watch her dance the tarantella at local theaters. Even though she died penniless back East, her memory is bright in Grass Valley, where her home now houses the Nevada County Chamber of Commerce. The house, built in 1851, also holds a small museum. And Mark Twain, who wrote about Grass Valley, also performed in local theaters, drawing large crowds.

Hamilton Hall, where many came to enjoy Lola Montez and her flamboyant performances, circa 1860. Courtesy California State Library, California Section, Sacramento. (Neg. #9273)

Mark Twain and Lola Montez, the celebrities of Grass Valley. Courtesy California Room, Yuba County Library, Marysville.

Looking east of Main Street between Mill and South Auburn Streets in Grass Valley. In January 1874, tailings from the Brunswick Mine were brought by wagon to Main Street for paving. Miners and townspeople searched among the crushed rock for gold nuggets, and when some flecks of "color" were found it prompted a small Gold Rush right in Main Street. Courtesy Jim Johnson, Heritage Graphics, Grass Valley.

THE EMPIRE MINE, just outside Grass Valley, is considered to be the oldest and richest hardrock mine in California. Cornish miners from Cornwall, England, were brought here for their knowledge of hardrock mining. Their greatest contribution was the Cornish Pump, which was able to pump water from incredible depths. The mine operated for over 100 years at depths of 11,000 feet, and yielded some $100 million in gold from its rock (gold prices in 1914). Today the Empire Mine, a State Historical Park, with the beautiful rock cottage made from the mining tailings, is open year around. The Cornish immigrants became a great influence in the town. At one time they made up 85% of the population. The Cornish miners often would take Cornish pasties, little meat pies that were carried in tin pails, to the mines for their mid-day meals. Today many of the town's markets and cafes serve these tasty legacies. Each Christmas, special Cornish festivities and celebrations draw tourists from all over the state.

The Omaha Mine, near Grass Valley. Courtesy California State Library, McIntire Collection. (Neg. #20,988)

Empire mining crew, circa 1890. Courtesy Searls Museum and Nevada County Historical Society, Nevada City.

Lyman Gilmore, Jr., right, and his brother, Charles Gilmore., in front of a very early plane. It is said that the dog often flew with them. Courtesy Nevada County Historical Society and Searls Museum.

AN UNUSUAL character in Grass Valley's history is Lyman Gilmore, Jr., who along with others, claimed to have built and flown a 32-foot steam powered aircraft in May 1902, before the Wright brothers' historic flight in December 1903. Gilmore's records showed a set of monoplane plans dated April 1898, and documented to have been built about 1903. But most of the records that might have verified his historic feat were lost in a fire in 1930. Sometime between 1905 and 1912 an airfield was built in Grass Valley, and the Gilmore Airship Company was incorporated. Many early pilots recall flying in and out of the airstrip, crediting this field with being one of the first in the West. The Lyman Gilmore school now stands on the site of the historic airfield.

There is no question that Gilmore was a true aviation pioneer. He promoted an air service linking cities throughout the United States, and he continued to design planes that proved dependable. In the 1930s Charles A. Lindberg signed a certificate from the Daniel Guggenheim Fund for the Promotion of Aviation which was presented to Gilmore for his efforts in "contributing to the establishment of a nationwide system of transportation by air." Grass Valley's Lyman Gilmore, Jr. can surely be called California's first aviator.

GRASS VALLEY RESOURCES

POINTS OF INTEREST
Empire Mine - (916) 271-8522 - A 784-acre park with tours and picnic areas
North Star Mining Museum - 10933 Allison Ranch Road
Grass Valley Museum - (916) 272-8188, the Old St. Mary's Convent Church
Driving or Walking Tours- Maps available at Chamber of Commerce
Historic Holbrook Hotel - 212 W. Main Street, (916) 273-1353
The Owl Inn - (916) 273-0526 - 134 Mill Street
The Lola Montez House - 248 Mill Street, today is the Grass Valley Chamber of Commerce (916) 273-4667
The Union Square Building - 151 Mill Street, today is a restaurant
Emmanuel Episcopal Church - 245 South Church Street
Nevada County Chamber of Commerce - 1-800-752-6222 (Ca.) 1-800-521-2075 (out of state)
Golden Gate Saloon Hotel - (916) 272-1989
Bret Harte Inn - Main Street, (916) 272-9097, today is a home for senior citizens

FESTIVALS
Miner's Picnic - Empire Mine State Park - first weekend in June
Summer Bluegrass Festival - Third weekend in June (916) 273-6217
Music in The Mountains - Sixteen days in June, check with Chamber of Commerce
Nevada County Fair - Last weekend in August
Cornish Christmas - Third and fourth weekends in November and first three weekends in December
Oktoberfest - First weekend in October at the Nevada County Fairgrounds in Grass Valley
Sierra Festival of The Arts - June, check with Chamber of Commerce.
Draft Horse Classic and Harvest Festival - September at the County Fairgrounds (916) 273-6217

SHOPPING & FARM PRODUCTS
Nevada County Certified Grower's Market - Grass Valley Fairgrounds on Saturday (June - October)
Roy's Tree Farm - 14446 Ott Way, berries, apples, & Christmas trees
Caroline's - 128 S. Auburn Boulevard - fruit, nuts, cheeses, grains and coffee
Belle Haven - (916) 273-8546. (July - September) apples and cat fishing
Pete Browne - (916) 273-2909, Christmas trees and wreaths
Giardina Orchards - (916) 272-7051 or 273-6571, (September - October) apples
Good Thyme Gardens - (916) 268-1016 - herbs and vegetables, mail order and gift packs
Sun Smile Farms - (916) 273-6507, cherries, peaches, apples
Wolf Mountain Trees and Pumpkins - (916) 268-3969, trees, crafts, pumpkins
Mt. Olive Tree Farm - (916) 346-8128, (October-December) trees and persimmons
Farmer's Market - Nevada County Fairgrounds on Wednesday August - October and Saturday June - October

BED AND BREAKFAST INNS & LODGES
Annie Horan's - 415 W. Main Street, (916) 272-2418
Domike's Inn - 220 Colfax Avenue (916) 273-9010
Golden Ore House - 448 S. Auburn Street, (916) 272-6870
Murphy's Inn - 318 Neal Street, (916) 273-6873
Swan - Levine House - 328 S. Church Street, (916) 272-1873

CEDAR RIDGE

CEDAR RIDGE once was only a farm house marking a stop and load location for the Nevada County Narrow Gauge Railroad, connecting neighboring Nevada City and Grass Valley to another mining town, Colfax. The landmark changed names from Kress's Summit to Cedar Crest before the name of Cedar Ridge was finalized. This exceptionally beautiful small community with a population of 1,309 is only a few miles east of Grass Valley. During the autumn, the entire ridge comes alive with spectacular fall color.

The Nevada County Narrow Gauge Railroad, circa 1920. The little train, known as "Never Come, Never Go," traveled over high trestles and narrow bridges, up steep hillsides, around dangerous curves, through dark tunnels and beautiful valleys, passing busy gold mines and bustling lumber mills. The train brought circus performers to town each year, delivered theater troupes to their stages, took townspeople to Sunday picnics, and carried patriotic sightseers to meet General Grant's train, Teddy Roosevelt's train, and Herbert Hoover's train as each one passed through Colfax. The narrow gauge railroad train ran from 1876 to 1942 when highway transportation became too competitive. Today the scenic Highway 174 follows this once vital railroad route. Courtesy Nevada County Historical Society and Searls Museum, Nevada City.

CEDAR RIDGE RESOURCES

Greenhorn - Rollins Lake Campground - Off Highway 174 on Greenhorn Road, (916) 346-2212

Orchard Springs - Rollins Lake Campground - Off Highway 174 on Orchard Springs Road, (916) 346-2212

NEVADA CITY

NEVADA CITY, about 40 miles east of Marysville on Highway 49, the Mother Lode Highway, is a twin city to Grass Valley. With 10,000 residents in the 1850s, Nevada City was the largest and most prosperous mining town in California. This fame later passed to its neighbor. By 1867 the population of Nevada City was about 3,500, while Grass Valley claimed 6,000 residents. First known as Coyoteville and Deer Creek Diggins, the town called Nevada (Spanish for snowy or snow-covered) added City to its name when the new state to the east chose or stole the name "Nevada." Today the county seat has 2,855 people, but Nevada County itself is one of the fastest growing counties in California.

A legendary figure who opened a business in Nevada City in 1854 was the sophisticated beauty, Madame Eleanora Dumont of New Orleans. She owned the "Vingt-et-Un" (French for twenty-one), a finely furnished and carpeted gambling saloon for only well-behaved and well-groomed men. She served champagne instead of whiskey, and she dealt the cards herself. Her establishment was open 24 hours a day, and she quickly gained the admiration and respect of her patrons. The slight growth of fuzz on her upper lip gave her the affectionate nickname of "Madame Moustache." She eventually left Nevada City, lost her fortune, and, penniless, committed suicide. But the gamblers and bartenders who had befriended the poor woman saw to it that she had a decent funeral, and a burial in a good cemetery, rather than in a pauper's grave.

Today Nevada City is a well-restored town with historic buildings housing unique shops and beautiful Victorian houses lining gas-lamp lit streets. During the month of December each year the historic mining town comes alive with Victorian Christmas activities, horse-drawn carriage rides, costumed carolers, spirited libations, and festive foods.

Main Street, Nevada City, circa 1852. Courtesy California State Library, McCurry Collection. (Neg. #4451)

Going from a tent town to quick-put-together clapboard shanties, Nevada City was constantly ablaze with uncontrolled fires. In 1856, a well-equipped fire fighting system was established, and soon became one of the best fire departments in the Mother Lode Country. Firehouse # 1, built in 1861, became a museum in 1940. Courtesy Nevada County Historical Society and Searls Museum, Nevada City.

Nevada City, circa 1893. Courtesy California State Library, California Section. (Neg. #6628)

NEVADA CITY is a quaint town with true historic character. Built on a series of hills, the town planned its streets to radiate out from the center like spokes of a wagon wheel. The maze of winding streets actually follows the old mule paths leading to the mining camps. Like many boom towns, this one was built of wood and canvas, and was a virtual tinderbox. In March 1851 a $1 million fire gutted the town, destroying 150 houses and numerous business buildings. Only rain and snow delayed the rebuilding of the Queen City of the Northern Mines. One new structure built in the early 1850s was the Yuba Canal Building, California's first major water company and forerunner of Pacific Gas and Electric Company. The old stone and brick building is used today by the Nevada City Chamber of Commerce.

Nevada City's gabled, steepled and slanted rooftops rise skyward to meet the clear, fresh mountain air of this beautifully maintained Sierra town. The National Hotel, built in 1854, the oldest continuously operated hotel in California, is one reason why this charming town has been designated a Historical Preservation District. Even during the height of its gold mining days, Nevada City was never known as a particularly rough town. Its theaters, museums, churches, and fine houses are evidence of the residents' long-standing appreciation of refinement, even elegance. The Nevada Theater, built in 1865, is the oldest theater still in existence in California. Today this queen city still has a high regard for the fine arts and theater.

NEVADA CITY RESOURCES

POINTS OF INTEREST
Chamber of Commerce - 132 Main Street (916) 265-2692
Miner's Foundry Cultural Center - 328 Spring Street, (916) 265-5804
Firehouse #1 Museum - 214 Main Street
Searls Historical Library - Built in 1872 for Niles Searl's law office. 1 pm - 4 pm, (916) 265-5910,
National Hotel - 211 Broad Street (916) 265-4551
South Yuba Independence Trail - Highway 49 (916) 272-3823 (first wheelchair wilderness trail)
Friar Tuck's Restaurant - 111 N. Pine Street (Swiss and French Fondue)
The Apple Fare - 307 Broad Street (916) 265-5458
Walking or Riding Tours of Historical Nevada City - Maps available Chamber of Commerce
Nevada City Brewery - Searls Ave.
Nevada City Winery - Spring Street
Teddy Bear Castle - 431 Broad Street

FESTIVALS
International Teddy Bear Convention - First weekend in April, (916) 265-5040
Annual House & Garden Tour - Third weekend in April
Music in The Mountains - June, check with Chamber of Commerce
Victorian Christmas - (916) 265-2692, Wednesday and Sunday evenings in December
Tour of Nevada City Bicycle Classic - Father's Day weekend in June (916) 265-2692
Constitution Day Parade - (916) 265-2692 - September (Nevada City designated as one of the nation's 15
   bi-centennial cities)
Winefest and Grape Stomp - (916) 265-5040

BED AND BREAKFAST INNS
Flume's Inn - 317 S. Pine (916) 265-9665
Red Castle Inn - 109 Prospect Avenue, (916) 265-5135
Piety Hill Inn - 523 Sacramento Street, (916) 265-2245
National Hotel - 211 Broad Street, (916) 265-4551
Downey House - 517 West Broad Street, (916) 265-2815
Grandmeres Inn - 449 Broad Street, (916) 265-4660
Palley Place - 12766 Nevada City Highway, (916) 265-5427
The Parsonage - 427 Broad Street, (916) 265-9478
Le Petit Chateau - 309 Commercial Street, (916) 265-6092
The Kendell House - (916) 265-0405

CAMPGROUNDS & RV PARKS
Scott's Flat Lake - 18849 Highway 20 - (916) 265-5302
Bowman National Forest - (916) 265-4538
Canyon Creek, Jackson Creek, Skillman, White Cloud, and Findley Campgrounds, (916) 265-4538
Gene's Pine Aire Campground - (916) 265-2832
Grizzly Creek Campground - (916) 265-3844
Grouse Ridge, Indian Springs, Jackson Point, Pass Creek, Skillman Flat and Woodcamp Campgrounds -
   (916) 265-4531

WASHINGTON

THIS VESTIGE of an old mining town is about 20 miles east of Nevada City, off scenic Highway 20. It was one of the first mining camps in the area, with some 3,000 men working the streams. A claim along a creek or the South Fork of the Yuba River was considered poor if it did not produce at least an ounce of gold a day per man. After the miners moved on, the Chinese sifted through the debris left behind or abandoned by the earlier miners. Many times they recovered as much as or more gold than those before them. Washington, through the years, has produced various ores including gold, asbestos, chrome, copper and lead. The Red Ledge Mine donated its old bell to the town to be placed in front of the Post Office, to ring when the mail comes in.

Washington, once alive with the excitement of the search for gold, today is not much more than a tourist attraction with about 250 full-time residents. But gold fever runs deep, and this area still lures those who dream of wealth. The River Rest Campground shows films on gold panning.

Chinatown in Washington, circa 1890. Courtesy Nevada County Historical Society and Searls Museum, Nevada City.

WASHINGTON RESOURCES

Washington Hotel - Built in 1856
Kohler Building - Built in 1854 from limestone
Brimskill Building - Built in 1849 and said to be the oldest structure in Nevada County
Alpha - Omega Lookout - East of Washington on Highway 20 overlooking the historic mines
Annual Chicken BBQ - Labor Day weekend
Annual Easter Day Picnic
River Rest Trailer Park & Campground - 13 miles east of Nevada City off Highway 20, (916) 265-4306
Gene's Pine - Aire Campgound - 20 miles north east of Nevada City off Highway 20, (916) 265-2832

Left: A mining camp near Washington used the hydraulic elevator to wash mountainsides away in order to expose gold ore, late 1800s. Courtesy Community Memorial Museum, Yuba City.

The Washington Hotel on Main Street, built in 1856, still stands in a mountain town that has changed little over the years. Its saloon is much as it was when miners patronized the place and paid their tab in gold. Sandra Shepherd, photographer.

NORTH SAN JUAN

NORTH SAN JUAN is a surprise when it just pops up suddenly from nowhere along the old Gold Rush trail, Highway 49, ten miles north of Nevada City. It was the main mining settlement on what is called the San Juan Ridge, reporting some 10,000 residents during the early days. The town took pride in its beautiful orchards, vineyards and gardens. Today this sleepy little landmark, with less than 400 residents, keeps mostly to itself, remembering the struggle and adventure of the days when mining and lumbering were at their peak. Campers, fishermen, hunters and historic explorers are drawn to the Gold Rush trails and the breathtaking Sierra Nevada Range.

North San Juan was called just San Juan until 1857, when the Post Office added North to the name to distinguish it from San Juan in San Benito County. It was not a Spanish town, but rather a bustling hamlet of workers of the local hydraulic mining operations, which left almost unbelievable erosion along the entire San Juan Ridge.

A nearby town, nearly forgotten, is French Corral, named for the corral built by a Frenchman in 1849 for the mule train beasts. French Corral is where the state's first long distance phone lines were strung. Installed in 1877 by the Milton Mining and Water Company, the lines extended to their company headquarters in French Lake, some 60 miles distant.

Two miles beyond French Corral is the famous Bridgeport covered bridge, built in 1862, the longest single span covered bridge in the United States. It was built by David I. Wood across the South Fork of the Yuba River and was used by freight trains carrying supplies to the Northern mines. Between 1901 and 1971 it was open to public use until it was determined unsafe.

North San Juan, 1860s. The water flume, carrying water for hydraulic mining, is suspended over Main Street. Courtesy of Nevada County Historical Society and Searls Museum.

View of North San Juan, 1880s. The open pastures were used for grazing cattle and horses. Courtesy Searls Museum and Nevada County Historical Society, Nevada City.

NORTH SAN JUAN RESOURCES

The Nevadacan Museum - 26195 Sweetland Museum Trail (916) 292-3477

Moonshine Campground - 14097 Moonshine Road, near Camptonville (916) 288-3585

Willow Creek Campgrounds - 17548 Highway 49, (916) 288-3456

French Corral - Pleasant Valley Road turnoff from Highway 49

Bridgeport - Located two miles from French Corral.

Main Street, San Juan, 1930s, with one of the telephone poles for California's first long distance phone line. Courtesy California State Library, Sacramento, the Stellman Collection.

165

NORTH BLOOMFIELD & MALAKOFF DIGGINS

THIS HISTORIC, restored ghost town, 15 miles northeast of Nevada City, was first called Humbug in 1851 for its unlucky mining. In 1857 the town was renamed North Bloomfield. During the days of hydraulic mining some 1,229 people lived here. Hydraulic mining equipment consisted of large fire hoses with jet-like nozzles to force a high-pressure water stream—created by diverting a river— out against a mountain cliff 24 hours a day. A 9-inch nozzle squirted 30,000 gallons of water per minute. This expensive yet profitable method for finding gold replaced the panning and sluice box methods used by earlier miners. Today the North Bloomfield is a State Historic Park, with just a handful of townsfolk living in the vicinity.

Malakoff Diggins was thought to be the richest of all California's hydraulic mining operations. It produced metal for the world's largest gold bar, weighing 510 pounds, and worth about $200,000. Hydraulic mining tore away nearly half of the mountain, leaving a 1,600 acre pit, 7,000 feet long, 3,000 feet wide, and 600 feet deep. Although the operation ran only from 1866 to 1884, it was responsible for washing out 30 million yards of gravel, leaving an eerie, yet awesome cavity sometimes described as a miniature Grand Canyon.

Malakoff Diggins hydraulic excavation, the most colossal in the Sierras, used wooden flumes to bring water down the mountainside from nearby streams. The three-foot-deep flume was over a thousand feet long and stood suspended up to six feet in the air.

Hydraulic mining. Courtesy California Room, Yuba County Library, Marysville.

People standing inside a water flume, 1900. The amount of lumber required to build such a flume was staggering. Courtesy Yuba Feather Historical Association, Forbestown.

NORTH BLOOMFIELD AND MALAKOFF DIGGINS

Malakoff Diggins State Historic Park - (916) 265-2740
Malakoff Diggins Historic Park Homecoming - (916)- 267-2692 -June
Grizzly Creek Campground - Highway 49 to Tyler Foote Road then to Tyler Foote Crossing, (916) 265-3844

CAMPTONVILLE

CAMPTONVILLE, with a population of less than 500, lies off Highway 49 on the road to Downieville. Named after blacksmith Robert Campton, this town too played a big part in the history of the gold mining era. In 1852, Camptonville became a central supply depot for the San Juan Ridge mining camps. In 1878 a local resident, Lester Pelton, invented the famous Pelton Wheel, a water-driven wheel used for mining gold. Its efficiency and power were remarkable; the Pelton Wheel generated 1,000 horsepower and turned at a rate of 70 miles per hour. The split-bucket water-powered iron wheel was so versatile and powerful that it was used to grind sausage as well as mountains. Pelton's wheel, patented and manufactured in various sizes, revolutionized the world-wide water power systems and was exported to such places as South America, Norway, Germany, China, and Japan.

Another creative gesture from Camptonville residents was the construction in 1853 of a bowling alley made from half a tree trunk cut with a whipsaw. Camptonville, with a population of 1,500, was a popular overnight stop for mountain travelers along the toll road to the county seat of Marysville. A well-liked resident who was a driver for the mountain stage line and also an agent for Well Fargo was old "Bull" Meek. He claimed never to have been robbed, as were many other stagecoach drivers, in all the years he worked the mining trails. It has been suggested that the women at the Downieville bordello, whose supplies were delivered by "Bull," used their influence on the "bad men" of the region.

Camptonville, circa 1915. The tall building at left center is the Odd Fellows Hall. Courtesy California Room, Yuba County Library, Marysville.

Camptonville school, a surprisingly elegant building with four stairways, circa 1915. Courtesy California Room, Yuba County Library, Marysville.

CAMPTONVILLE RESOURCES

The Pelton Wheel Monument
A Pelton Wheel - Stands in front of Nevada City's visitor's center
Campgrounds: Garden Point, Madrone Cove, School House and Upper Carlton Flat - (916)289-3216
Willow Creek Campground - 17548 Highway 49, (916) 288-3456
Tahoe National Forest Ranger Station - (916) 288-3231

ALLEGHANY

Ridge Road, off Highway 49, winds upward to the very remote mountain village of Alleghany. Perched on a slope some 40 miles from Nevada City, the little settlement of weathered clapboard houses and aged fences has single-lane roads going around the town, making driving courtesy a must. The town is much favored as a center for deer hunting and other outdoor sports.

The old camp town got its start when a group of Hawaiian sailors who had jumped ship to search for gold first settled here. Kanaka Creek, named after the Hawaiians, turned out to be their "river of gold." One of the most exciting strikes was the Original Sixteen To One Mine, established in 1896 and named for the campaign slogan of Presidential Candidate William Jennings Bryan, referring to the proposed gold to silver ratio for United States coinage. When the mine closed in 1965 it had produced in excess of $26 million in gold.

Another famous mine nearby, the Rainbow, was said to have yielded $60,000 in a single day. Alleghany claims to have had the highest grade of mined ore ever registered in the Mother Lode Country. Approximately $50 million in gold has been taken from the Alleghany hillsides. Legend tells of an Alleg-hany miner who "lifted" a few pieces of high grade ore from a mine between 1914-1915. Thirty years later he sent the company a registered letter with $2,700 in bills as payment for the "borrowed" ore. Somewhat surprising was the return address, from a man living in Sacramento.

H.L. Johnson, owner of the Tightner Mine in Alleghany, checking out the strata and gold veins, circa 1907. Courtesy California State Library, California Section. (Neg. # 8757)

Winter in Alleghany, 1930's. Today the remaining buildings of Alleghany, still clinging to the mountainside, are virtually inaccessible during hard winters. Courtesy Nevada County Historical Society and Searls Museum, Nevada City.

THE REBIRTH of the Original Sixteen to One Mine, one of the most productive and profitable gold mines in California's history, took place in January 1992. Forty-two years earlier, in 1950, Mike Miller's father had bought stock in the old mine. Years later Mike's interest in the historic mine began to grow. After he convinced share-holders that the mine was still viable and should be operated by the Original Sixteen to One Mine Corporation, repairs began on the neglected shafts. Metal detectors were introduced to locate the ore, and within nine months $1.3 million was found. Corporation president Miller proposed to the new crew that if they would work for reduced wages, they would get a percentage of the recovered gold. Mr. Miller reports that the gold pulled from a recently found pocket was so rich that most was melted and poured directly into bars with no need for milling. One day's bonus for each crewman has amounted to up to $700.

Fifty-two sacks of gold from the Original Sixteen to One Mine, ready for shipment to the Citizens Bank in Nevada City, circa 1910. Guarding the treasure are George Bailey, left, and Eddie Morgan. Courtesy Mike Miller and the Original Sixteen to One Mine.

The Original Sixteen to One Mine crew, circa 1916. The mine brought men from all parts of California to work one of the world's richest veins of gold. Many grandchildren of the original crew are still shareholders, who incorporated the mine and have leased it out for the past 25 years. Courtesy of Mike Miller and the Original Sixteen to One Mine.

GOODYEARS BAR

GOODYEARS BAR lies between Camptonville and Downieville just off Highway 49. Named for brothers Andrew and Miles Goodyear, who settled the area in 1852, this tiny speck of a mountain village, studded with mighty pines, was once a bustling mining camp, the first of two established in the rugged mountains along the North Fork of the Yuba River. The prospectors who forged their way to these high mountains were rugged and determined characters. It took strong will and stamina to withstand the severe winters, the hardship and isolation. Many dreamed of finding their fortunes, but failed. Between 1850 and 1852, Goodyears Bar was almost as populous as nearby Downieville. But when news of a Canadian gold strike spread, many people left for the north. Some of the persistent settlers stayed on and realized true riches: the incomparable beauty of land around them.

One forty-niner, John Louis Jordan, quoted in an article in *The World*, May 2, 1965, wrote of Goodyears Bar, "We are surrounded with a romantic scenery here, the lofty peaks rearing up all around us, covered with beautiful evergreen trees—and at the same time covered with snow—which makes it all glistening in the hot broiling sun. I have walked over snow banks here in the latter part of June, five to ten feet deep, when at the same time the sun would be uncomfortable hot."

One of many gold prospectors transporting supplies to camp.
Courtesy California Section, California State Library, Sacramento. (Neg. # 103)

GOODYEARS BAR RESOURCES

Old School House - Today is the Community Club House
Historic Hotel
Original Goodyears Ranch - Privately owned
"R" Place Trailer Park

DOWNIEVILLE

DOWNIEVILLE, perched on two hillsides and straddling the Yuba and Downie Rivers 50 miles northeast of Nevada City, sits near Sierra Butte. The town still looks as it did in the mining days, with narrow streets and a downtown with old stone and brick buildings standing alongside weathered wood-frame structures flanked by wooden sidewalks. Downieville, surely one of the most charming Gold Rush towns in Northern California, was named for the Scotsman, Major William Downie, a storekeeper from Bullard's Bar who built one of the first cabins in the gold camp. In 1850 it was reported that miners were removing up to two pounds of gold a day each from the North Fork of the Yuba River. A year later a 26½-pound nugget worth $8,000 (about $1.5 million at today's gold prices) was found on the river's banks.

Elaborate flumes and pumps were used along the river between Downieville and Good-years Bar to divert the water from its bed, thus enabling the miners to work the exposed gravel. Siphons were also used to prevent water seepage that hampered any search for riches. Even though millions in gold were recovered from the streams, rivers and mountainsides, only a small percentage of miners really struck it rich.

A Downieville street with prospectors loading up supplies for the rugged trip into the surrounding hills in search for gold. This was a very familiar sight throughout many years of gold prospecting. Courtesy California State Library, California Section, Sacramento. (Neg. # 5065)

The St. Charles Hotel in Downieville was a famous social center in the 1860s. Courtesy California State Library, California Section, Sacramento. (Neg. # 5066)

DOWNIEVILLE was notorious as a hanging town. The original gallows still stands, and was the site of the controversial hanging on July 4, 1851 of a Mexican dance hall girl named Juanita, who stabbed a miner she claimed molested her. She was the first woman to be hanged in California. It has taken Downieville, the quaint little town of 400 people, many years to live down the stigma of the town's decision.

Downieville in the 1930s, reflecting then and now the look of yesteryear. Courtesy California State Library, California Section, the Stillman Collection. (Neg. #3446)

DOWNIEVILLE RESOURCES

Sierra County Museum - Main Street, formerly a Chinese Gambling House
Catholic Church - Built in 1858
Methodist Episcopal Church - Built in 1865, oldest Protestant Church in continuous use in California
Herschfeldter Building
Craycroft Building - Built in 1852 and once was a saloon with a 70 foot bar
Lions' Memorial - Near the forks in the river, displays of old mining relics
Gallows - Beside Sierra County Courthouse site of the hanging of Juanita, a dance hall girl
Sierra Skies RV Park - Highway 49- (916) 862-1166
Downieville Ranger District - For camping areas (916) 288-3231
Miners Day Weekend - August, (915) 862-1431
Holiday On Main - December, (916) 862-1431
Sierra Shangri - La - (Bed & Breakfast Inn)–3 miles north of town on Highway 49, (916) 289-3455
Sierra County Chamber of Commerce - (916) 289-3560
Tahoe National Forest Ranger Station - (916)–288-3231

BIBLIOGRAPHY

–Browne, Juanita Kennedy, *Nuggets of Nevada County History.* Nevada City, CA, Nevada County Historical Society

–Colebered, Frances, *Hidden Country Villages of California.* San Francisco, CA, Chronicle Books, 1977

–Delay, Peter J., *History of Yuba and Sutter Counties.* Los Angeles, CA, Historic Record Co., 1924

–Duffy, Jr., William J., *The Sutter Basin and Its People.* The Printer, 1972

–Ellis, W.T., *Memories, My Seventy Years in the Romantic County of Yuba California.* Eugene, OR, University of Oregon, 1939

–Gridley Junior Women's Club, *Gridley Centennial - Pictorial History Book, 1850-1900.* Publisher and date unknown

–Gordon, Marjorie, *Changes in Harmony.* Northridge, CA, Windsor Publications, 1988

–Hendrix, Louis, *The Sutter Buttes.* Publisher unknown, 1981

–Hurst, Stephen G., *This Is My Own, My Native Land.* Independent Press, 1956

–Jackson, Joseph Henry, illustrated by E.H. Suydam, *Anybody's Gold - The Story of California's Mining Towns.* New York,

–Kirsch, Robert & William S. Murphy, *West of the West.* New York, E.P. Dutton & Co., Inc. 1967

–Johnson, Wilmeth M., *The Town of Maxwell - From the Beginning 1878 to Present.* Publisher unknown, 1981

–Lague, Jim, *Forbes of Forbestown and Stories and Poems by Jennie Forbes.* Publisher unknown, 1986

–Mansfield, George C., *History of Butte County.* Los Angeles, CA, Historic Record Co., 1918

–Milton, Milo, editor, *Pictures of Gold Rush California.* Citadel Press, Inc. 1967

–Nadeau, Remi, *Ghost Towns and Mining Camps of California.* Los Angeles, CA, The Ward Richie Press, 1965

–Roske, Ralph J. *Every Man's Eden - A History of California.* New York, Macmillan Co., N.Y. and Collier- Macmillan, 1968.

–Sacramento Chamber of Commerce, *The Romance of California.* Publisher unknown, 1938

–Seagraves, Anne, *Women of the Sierra.* Lakeport, CA, Wesanne Enterprises, 1990

–Slyter, Robert J. & Grace J. Slyter, *Historical Notes of the Early Washington, Nevada County, California Mining District.* Publisher and date unknown

–Sullivan, Janet and MaryJane Zall, *The Survivors: Existing Homes and Buildings of Yuba and Sutter Counties' Past.,* Publisher unknown, 1974

–Thompson and West, *History of Sutter County, California with Illustrations, 1879.* Reproduction published by Howell-North Books, 1974

–Talbitzer, Bill, *Echoes of the Gold Rush.* Publisher unknown, 1985

–Talbitzer, Bill, *Lost Beneath the Feather.* Publisher unknown, 1963

–Talbitzer, Bill, *The Gandydancers.* Publisher unknown, 1973

–Teets, Bob and Shelby Young, *Rivers of Fear - The Great California Flood of 1986.* Terra Alta, W. V., C.R. Publications, Inc., 1986

–Wagner, Jack R., *Gold Mines of California.* Berkeley, Howell-North Books, 1970

—Wrisley, Kristin, photographs by Charles Moore, *The Mother Lode - A Pictorial Guide to California's Gold Rush Country.*, San Francisco, CA, Chronicle Books, 1983

—Workman, Lottie Lathrop, *Memories of Hammonton.* Publisher unknown, date unknown

—Winther, Oscar O., *Via Western Express and Stagecoach.* Palo Alto, CA, Stanford University Press, 1938

—Worthington, Carol, *Black Pioneers of Yuba County.* Publisher unknown, 1987

—Yeadon, David, *Exploring Small Towns 2. Northern California.* Los Angeles, CA, The Ward Ritchie Press, 1973

—Young, Helen D., *Arbuckle and College City.* Fresno, CA, Pioneer Publishing, date unknown

—Yuba County Historical Society Commission, *The History of Yuba County.* 1976

—*Dogtown Territorial Quarterly,* 1990-1992

—*Golden Grain Harvest, The California Story.* Video produced by Rice Industry Committee, with cooperation from DuPont Agricultural Products, date unknown

—*Sierra Heritage.* November-December 1992

—*The World Almanac and Book of Facts.* World Almanac, 1992

INDEX

-Y-

Yahi Indians - 96
Yarick, A.H. - 46
Yates, Herman - 50
Yates, Nela - 50
Yolo County - 46
Yosemite Falls - 101
Young, Larry - 125
Young Life Organization - 138
Yuba City - 16-23, 70, 76
Yuba City Grammar School - 20
Yuba Consolidated Goldfields - 11, 93
Yuba County - 3, 20, 125, 134, 146
Yuba County Courthouse - 6
Yuba County Hospital - 12
Yuba County Library - viii
Yuba River - 2, 4, 14, 15, 21, 146-147,
    162, 164, 169-172
Yuba-Sutter Gun Club - 8

-Z-

Zelkova Trees - 149
Zumwalt, I.G. - 37